An Interviewing Rhetoric

Thomas J. Roach, Ph.D.
Purdue University–Calumet

KENDALL/HUNT PUBLISHING COMPANY
4050 Westmark Drive   Dubuque, Iowa 52002

*To Ben –
my fellow
musician +
my friend.*

Dedicated to

Thomas Farrell
"The desert's quiet and Cleveland's cold"

Contents

Acknowledgements

All rhetorical theory and criticism has a lineage, and mine is Aristotle through Lloyd Bitzer through Thomas Farrell. Tom was my teacher and my good friend. He wrote essays in the service of public address.

I was already teaching interviewing when I took my first class with Tom in 1988. We had many discussions about interviewing and rhetoric over the years, and it was with his support that I began this project. I first assembled my chapters so I could print a copy for him to review. The file on my computer still reads "All Chapters Farrell." Regrettably, I gave him the manuscript, but we never had a chance to discuss it. I know what he thought of the ideas in this book, but I very much wanted to know if he thought it was well written.

Bruce Rismiller was the source and the inspiration for much of the material on the employment interview. The environment he created at the Carson Pirie Scott corporate offices was a laboratory for business communication strategies. His prowess as a mentor is only exceeded by his powers as an educator.

Lastly, I would like to thank my wife Susan for keeping me humble, honest, and grammatically correct.

Introduction

Many of the lessons contained in this manuscript were learned from my students. I remember Lisa Daugherty, James Kasper, and Julian Stryczak singing a Lou Reed song in my first Introduction to Interviewing class at Purdue University Calumet in 1987. I never had a class full of communication majors before; compared to my experience teaching English, this was out of control; I was afraid the department head would find out and tell me my students had taken over the classroom. Yet, my business leadership experience told me that participation was desirable, and we were having a *good* time! They were the beginning of a relationship I would have with all my students and the realization that teachers and students learn from one another.

Interviewing soon became my favorite class. Having worked in journalism, media relations, corporate employee communication, political campaign research and advertising, I had performed most types of interviews and felt more than qualified to teach the subject. But the classroom cycle of theory and practice coupled with constant student interaction and feedback caused me to reexamine everything.

Usually four or five interviews of five to eight minutes are conducted each day. The students and I observe. I take notes. Class is dismissed after the last interview, and I call the interviewers to the front of the room. One by one, I show them their grades and give them their feedback. Amazingly part and sometimes all of the class stays to hear the feedback. Occasionally a feedback session with a student turns into a group discussion with someone in the classroom telling the interviewer what questions might have been asked to extend a probing sequence. I had a student one semester, Regina Hurst, who regularly pulled a chair up to the table while I was giving feedback and, when I was done, told me what I missed.

Sometimes students would work an interview to the point where they could ask a question that caused the interviewee to think and soul-search for an answer. This became the main focus of my teaching. If someone got in just one good stop-them-in-their-tracks question, I gave him or her an A. I never thought an entire interview could take place on that level until I witnessed it. It was Jim Zaleski, Annie Curtis, and Reena Guernsey who broke through the probing barrier for me in the Spring semester of 1992. Jim wanted to sign up for class after missing the first week. I told him no; I had a policy. Jim, always a bargainer, appealed to my sense of competition when he suggested he get notes from someone else in the class, sit in on the second week of lectures, and then take the first test with everyone else. If he didn't get the highest score in the class, he would go quietly; if he did get the high score, I had to let him register. I took him up on it, and I wrote a particularly difficult exam. Annie was the smartest student in the department, and everyone knew it. Jim borrowed Annie's notes and topped the class by scoring 97, beating out Annie at 94. The impact on the class was remarkable. We started live in-class interviews the next week. Jim, now quite full of himself, volunteered to go first. His radical effort to prepare for the test must have resulted in his making connections between theory and practice that none of my students had made before. His interview had deep meaningful probing from start to finish. I was amazed. I gave him an A+ and told him it was the best probing interview I had ever seen. Annie volunteered to go first the next night. I impishly selected Jim for her interviewee, and she took him apart. After class I told them she topped Jim's interview, and Jim agreed with me. Reena, who I had barely noticed, got caught up in the competition. She did her interview the third night and topped Annie. As they say in sports, she was unconscious. I have seen over 1,000 live interviews where students interview subjects whom I have randomly selected, and I have never seen one more fluid and incisive than Reena's. Hers is the model interview that this book attempts to describe.

Students also taught me lessons about being interviewed. Adrienne Viramontes and Amy Temple knew their minds and had no constraints about expressing themselves. I discovered them in Introduction to Public Relations and actually recruited them for my interviewing class. They were more aggressive as interviewees than the other students were as interviewers. By volunteering unexpected information and throwing questions back at the interviewer, they dominated the exchange. My focus had been teaching interviewers to work with interviewees who were not volunteering information. Watching Adrienne and Amy I learned how much the interviewee could manipulate the interview and that interviewers needed to be prepared for that as well. At the other end of the spectrum, Pat Mellon exemplified the thoughtful, cooperative response. If Reena is the model interviewer, Pat is the model interviewee. She showed how effective an interview could be, even with an uninspiring topic, if the interviewee made an honest effort to find the most meaningful emotional and intellectual response.

I never let an interviewer pick an interviewee. My only exception was a good one. In an evening class with students mostly in their mid 20s or early 30s, one young woman who sat in the front of the class was particularly talkative and forthcoming. In class discussions she revealed things about herself that most of us didn't want to know. I began to avoid calling on her, and I dreaded having to select her to be someone's interviewee. A sullen young man who sat in the back said very little, but when he did speak, he was sharp witted. He seemed skeptical of me, the class, and the world. Think of the two of them as James Dean and a young Jane Fonda. I called on James to come to the front of the room to conduct his interview before I had decided who the interviewee would be. It was a tough call; I hesitated. James stopped as he passed Jane's desk. "I want to interview her." I was horrified. Before I could speak, they whisked their way to the table and were waiting for me to tell them to start. Curiosity got the better of me, and I hit my stopwatch. He began the interview with a highly personal question which she immediately answered. Her answer challenged him by giving him more information than he asked for and certainly more than any of us needed to hear, but he took the challenge and came back with a tough follow-up. The interview developed at a break-neck pace right to the very last response. It was spellbinding. If the building caught fire, I don't think they would have stopped, and I don't think any of us would have left.

Another class had Sister Evelyn, Wendy Rivas, and Caleb Johnson. Sister Evelyn already had a degree and was much older than the other students who were mostly in their early 20s. Wendy reminded me of Adrienne and Amy. She was smart, analytical, and not afraid to tell say what was on her mind. Caleb was also very bright, but he was cagy. He claimed once that he received As and Bs in most of his classes without ever opening a book. He wasn't lazy; he thought it was a game. When I select interviewees I sometimes try to match aggressive interviewers with non-aggressive interviewees and vice versa. The reticent interviewees make interviewers work harder, and talkative interviewees can keep the interview alive for a weak interviewer. Logically, I selected Sister Evelyn to be interviewed by Wendy. It was an employment interview, and I was right in assuming that Sister Evelyn didn't have much to talk about. Wendy, however, had verbal skills considerably more acute than I had imagined. When Sister Evelyn said she had no career goals, Wendy wanted to know why. When Sister Evelyn said she never thought about it, Wendy wanted to know why she never thought about it. Sister Evelyn was trying to cooperate, but she couldn't satisfy Wendy's questions, and Wendy kept pushing her back into a psychological corner. If it were a prize fight, I would have called a technical knockout and stopped it. A very long seven or eight minutes passed before it ended, and I was ashamed of myself for having put Wendy in a position where she had to push so hard, and having put Sister Evelyn in a position where she was being pushed. I tried to apologize after class, but Sister Evelyn didn't understand why. She took it as a learning experience and nothing more. When it came time for her interview, I selected Caleb as the interviewee. I thought Caleb might keep things going if Sister Evelyn didn't know what to ask. However, Sister Evelyn was every bit as aggressive and articulate as Wendy, except Sister Evelyn had an added advantage of never betraying her emotions. Her questions were always flat and kind, yet just as imposing as Wendy's. She took Caleb by surprise. He began contradicting himself and stumbling over his words. When Sister Evelyn was done, she casually got up and walked away, but I felt like we should have called for a gurney for poor Caleb. He has since gone to law school and begun a law practice. I will have to ask him some day if he has ever seen a cross-examination like the one Sister Evelyn gave him.

Some of what I learned from my students came outside the classroom. Shawn Platt and JT Mc Kee had an evening interviewing class. Shawn was a hotshot with a full time job and an "I dare you to teach me something" attitude. JT was a more serious student. He formed a study group and came to class well prepared. He practiced with and coached the other students in the study group and sometimes argued with me if one of them didn't get an A on an interview. One night Shawn, who was not in the study group, was randomly selected to conduct his interview. He asked only one primary question; everything that followed was a probing question that drove deeper into information gleaned from the previous answer. It was a tour de force of follow-up question asking. I gave him an A+ and let everyone know it. After class the three of us went out for a beer.

"How did you prepare for that?" JT asked Shawn.

"I didn't," Shawn said. He admitted he came to class unprepared, and when I selected him to go first, he only had time to write down one primary question. He knew that if he stopped probing, the interview would be over. JT was not amused, but Shawn's story provided a significant insight. Concentrating on the interviewee and being flexible are more important than a schedule of questions; in fact, the schedule of questions is probably counterproductive. Eventually I started teaching students to use an outline of topics that has not been written as questions and to ask as few primary questions as possible.

In *The Gorgias* Plato somewhat mockingly compares rhetoric with boxing, but in many ways it was an apt analogy. By most accounts Athenian citizens were competitively making and refuting arguments about every imaginable subject. The entire city was a forum, and students of rhetoric had the opportunity practice their skills everywhere they went. Over 2,000 years later, we still employ the rhetorical arts, but mostly now we do so in private. We author essays or articles, but are not present when they are read. We go into soundproof studios to record messages that are broadcast to millions of viewers and listeners with whom we have no meaningful interaction. Here in the interviewing classroom is an opportunity to rediscover what it is like to live with rhetoric. It can be a transformative learning experience, and it is one that I know is as rewarding for the teacher as it is for the student.

Chapter One

An Interviewing Rhetoric

Studying the Interview

Everyone reading this book is already an expert interviewer. We all have been asking and answering questions since we learned to speak. Each of us has a unique personality that takes advantage of certain strategic, stylistic, organizational, and vocal techniques. We may have very different approaches, but we all have ways of getting what we want when we need information. Studying the unconscious, spontaneous interviewing examples around us at home, at work, or with friends, is probably the best way to improve our understanding and our skills. The formal study of interviewing, then, is a companion to the accumulation of wisdom throughout the course of our lives. An interviewing book or class should add to our knowledge while at the same time helping to sort out subjective experiences and observations so they can be better understood and applied with greater precision and effectiveness.

Let us begin by looking at the common definition of interviewing. Generally it is considered a subcategory under communication where people ask and answer specific questions in professional settings. Journalists interview community leaders about upcoming events. Police interview witnesses and victims about crimes. Employers interview job applicants to gauge qualifications and compatibility. Students interview professors about tests. Triage nurses interview emergency room patients about their injuries. Clergy interview prenuptial couples about marriage. Social workers interview clients about their needs and resources. Marketing researchers interview consumers about their buying habits. Political strategists interview citizens about their voting preferences. In each of these examples, the interviewer and interviewee are aware that their verbal interaction constitutes an interview. Typically, we see interviews as self-conscious interludes, bracketed exceptions to the normal flow of our lives. Interviewing, however, is more than this.

In fact, almost all human communication calls for and responds to the communication of others. Questions and answers that are sometimes explicit, but most often implicit, fill our daily conversations. This is one of the secrets of professional scriptwriting. Fictional characters rarely give speeches; they mainly ask and answer questions. Authors who claim a script practically wrote itself probably discovered they might only need to invent a first line and then follow the natural logic of the dialogue. The next time you have a meal with the family, attend a meeting, or watch a sit-com or a movie, take notice of how much of the formal dialogue is straightforward question asking and answering. Then consider how much of the informal, non-question and answer dialogue around you is still a call and response. That is, try to notice how much of what we say is in response to what others have said. Stepping back and observing somewhat objectively, one realizes that almost everything we say to one another is part of a give-and-take dialogue.

The Rhetoric of Information Gathering

The body of theory through which we will study interviewing is called rhetoric. Good research and theory development should make the world less complicated, not more complicated. This is as true for communication as it is for physics. As a first step toward understanding and demystifying interviewing, it should be noted that even though communication has been taught in college classes for only about 50 years, it has been studied and written about under the name of rhetoric since ancient times. In classical Greece and Rome, rhetoric was divided into five canons: invention, arrangement, style, delivery, and memorization. In spite of all the recent evolutions of mass media, most communication can still be accounted for by the five canons of rhetoric, and it would be foolish to complicate matters with new methods of analysis and exposition when there is already a rich history of theory and practice upon which to build.

The names of the five canons of rhetoric are mostly self-explanatory. *Invention* refers to inventing a statement or argument. *Arrangement* refers to the arrangement of topics and subtopics. *Style* means the way we dress up what we say. Both arrangement and style are terms we learn when studying English. That is because the study of English is derived from the study of rhetoric. *Delivery* means the use of voice and gesture when we communicate. Students of interviewing may be familiar with delivery from speech classes. The study of speech also is derived from the ancient art of rhetoric. The last canon is memorization. *Memorization* can mean to commit to memory what one is about to say, but it is also a method of preparation. In classical times, one memorized the speeches of others to learn cadences of speech and habits of reason.

In classical Greece and Rome, rhetoric was preoccupied with public address—speechmaking. The object of all classical teaching was to help the speaker make the best argument. Interviewing, while it employs all the strategies and tactics of traditional rhetoric, is in many ways the opposite of speechmaking. Interviewing uses the canons of rhetoric to call for the arguments of others. While someone giving a speech must identify a topic, in interviewing the topic is supplied by the interviewer. This is because the listener and not the speaker controls the speaking situation. If the interviewer has a guide or a schedule of questions, then he or she also supplies the arrangement for the speaker. While both interviewer and interviewee each control their own use of style, the application of this canon is most influenced by the interviewer who sets the tone for the dialogue. Delivery is a particularly interesting subject for interviewing. In the interview, it is the audience which dominates and provides the motivation for the speaker. In this reversal of roles, listening, the opposite of delivery, becomes the preeminent concern. Memorization also plays a part in reverse. The burden of remembering is on the interviewer, not the speaker, although it is the speaker's memories and opinions that are the subject of the interview. Just as speakers have strategies to remember speeches they give, interviewers have strategies for remembering speeches they hear.

Dialectic

While rhetorical theorists in classical times did not have a general term for interviewing, they did define it more narrowly as dialectic. In ancient Greece dialectic was a way of reasoning and coming to an understanding of the truth by asking and answering questions. It has been argued that all logic and even all human knowledge are dialectical; that is, that the process by which we come to know things necessarily involves the asking and answering of questions. In its simplest form, we employ dialectic internally sometimes to reach conclusions or make decisions. When buying a car, for instance, one might ask oneself, "Which is more important, comfort, style, or economy?" If the answer is economy, the next question might be something like, "What is more important, fuel efficiency or the cost of the car?" Logically, if one drives long distances, and if gasoline is expensive enough, one might conclude that fuel efficiency is paramount, and that a hybrid car is worth the extra cost. Now, this dialogue could take place with someone else, or it could take place in one's head; either way it is still the asking and answering of questions. It is dialectic; and it is a kind of interview.

Significantly, for the ancient Greek philosophers, dialectic focused on contradiction and agreement. Almost all communication strives for agreement, but too few thinkers and speakers today understand the role of contradiction. Dialectic applied contradiction chiefly to test and find exception with an argument. Unlikely as it might seem, well applied contradiction in the dialectical process actually developed and, if merited, proved the argument. This is one of the most important lessons to be learned from our rhetorical past. Almost regardless of the parties and the situation, the interview is most useful when the interviewer tests and challenges accounts and ideas. Often people feel that to challenge someone's statement is an attempt to prove that he or she is wrong, but rhetorical tradition teaches us that it may also be the best way of proving someone is right.

Socrates, the fifth century BC philosopher, used a dialectic interviewing method to teach as he roamed the streets of Athens. He would ask questions of students and bystanders and then make them defend their answers. As they replied to his follow-up questions, Socrates led them sequentially through their own arguments, helping them understand where they were right or where they were wrong. He did this essentially by patiently challenging their answers and letting them discover the truth for themselves. Another technique that was part of Socrates' use of dialectic was to make a paradoxical or provocative statement that would cause the other party to ask him questions. Either way, Socrates was in control, and the question and answer process was maintained. Although few professors master this technique, it is called the Socratic teaching method, and it is still used today.

While no text of an actual Socratic dialogue exists, there are several fictionalized examples provided by his student Plato. Plato used Socrates as a character in dramatic scripts that were probably meant to be read. Plato would develop a philosophical thesis by creating a give-and-take dialogue between Socrates and the other characters. Sometimes Socrates asks the questions, and sometimes he makes statements that cause his listeners to ask questions. Frequently his questions lure the other speaker into making illogical statements which are indefensible. Ultimately, he leads a companion or a group of listeners to the point where they must come to the logical conclusion for themselves. Plato didn't write the dialogues to teach us the Socratic method but to teach philosophy, yet they provide wonderful examples of the dialectical rhetorical strategy we call the Socratic method. In this excerpt from "The Gorgias," Socrates asks questions and builds his argument around the answers of the reluctant Polus:

> *Socrates:* In the first place, are injustice and wrongdoing the greatest of evils?
>
> *Polus:* It seems so.
>
> *Socrates:* And has it further been shown that to be brought to justice is to be rid of this evil?
>
> *Polus:* It seems possible.
>
> *Socrates:* But not to be brought to justice ensures a continuance of this evil?
>
> *Polus:* Yes.
>
> *Socrates:* Wrongdoing, then, is merely the second greatest of evils; to do wrong and not be brought to justice is the first and greatest of all evils.

We can see that Polus has little role in what is a straightforward attempt to develop a thesis with questions. In the following excerpt, Socrates makes paradoxical statements that he knows will draw a series of questions from Polus. Polus has argued that orators are the most powerful people in the country because by using their rhetorical skills and persuading other citizens, they can confiscate property and banish or put to death anyone they please. Socrates contradicts Polus when he calls people with power "wretches" and later says that it is worse to cause an injustice than to suffer one. See how Polus, while trying to oppose Socrates' argument, ends up interviewing Socrates and actually helps Socrates develop his argument:

> *Polus:* Just exactly as though you, Socrates, would not choose to have the power to do what you thought best rather than not to have it! Just as though you wouldn't feel envy if you saw another man who had killed anyone he pleased, or robbed him, or put him in prison!
>
> *Socrates:* Do you mean justly or unjustly?
>
> *Polus:* Whichever it may be, isn't it enviable either way?
>
> *Socrates:* Hush, hush, my dear Polus!
>
> *Polus:* What's the matter?
>
> *Socrates:* We must never envy the unenviable or the wretched, but pity them.
>
> *Polus:* How's that? Is this your opinion of the condition of the men I mentioned?
>
> *Socrates:* How could it be otherwise?
>
> *Polus:* So whoever kills, and justly kills, anyone he judges proper seems to you to be wretched and pitiable?

Socrates: No, but scarcely enviable.

Polus: But didn't you just say that he was wretched?

Socrates: No, my friend, I was talking about the man who killed unjustly, and he is pitiable as well; but a man who kills justly is still unenviable.

Polus: Well, at any rate, there is no doubt that a man who is put to death unjustly is really pitiable and wretched.

Socrates: Less so than the man who kills him, Polus, and also less than the man who is put to death justly.

Polus: Now what on earth do you mean by that, Socrates?

Socrates: That to do injustice is the greatest of all evils.

Polus: What? Is it the greatest? Isn't to suffer injustice a greater evil?

Socrates: By no means.

Polus: So you'd prefer to suffer injustice rather than do it?

Socrates: For myself I should prefer neither; but if it were necessary for me either to do or suffer injustice, I should choose to suffer rather than do it.

In both examples, we see the question and answer technique of developing an argument. In the first passage, Socrates develops his argument with questions and in the second with answers. The second passage is particularly interesting because Socrates inverts the interviewer/interviewee roles, yet still maintains control of the dialogue.

A Contemporary Definition of the Interview

While one might argue that asking and answering questions is imbedded in most human communication, it is important to note that the formal interview has characteristics that separate it from other forms of communicative action. It is ***dialectical***, it is ***results oriented***, and it is ***spontaneous***.

Dialectical communication has a purpose. It drives toward discovering new information or drawing a conclusion. Dialectical communication is also somewhat of a contest. Those involved go back and forth adding to or challenging what has just been said. This is very different from communication that is not dialectical. Sometimes people ask questions while making what is called small talk. When we greet one another we often say "how are you?" This is rarely intended to be dialectical. The appropriate response is "Fine. How are you?" The words are uttered in the form of questions, but their purpose is to express goodwill. Unless you are talking to your doctor, if you respond to "How are you?" with a list of aches and pains you have missed the point.

The interview is not just dialectical in nature; it actually takes place between two parties. Usually there is an interviewer and an interviewee. The interviewer asks a question, the interviewee answers. This is an important distinction: the interview is one-on-one. There are powerful social and psychological pressures brought to bear when two people face one another and one of them asks a question. In most cases, the interviewee feels compelled to answer. If you don't believe this, the next time someone asks you a question face-to-face, try ignoring it.

This is not the case in a small or large group discussion, and certainly not when it comes to mass communication. It is much easier to change the subject or ignore a question in a small group where there are multiple parties with whom to interact. As the numbers increase, the practicality of question asking and answering decreases. One might say, what about a courtroom where many people are present, yet an attorney is nonetheless able to bring a great deal of compliance pressure to bear on a witness. The answer to this riddle is that the rules of courtroom procedure create a one-on-one relationship between the interviewer attorney and interviewee witness. The others present in the courtroom are merely observers. If however, the judge, the jury, and the other witnesses were all allowed to shout questions at the same time, the interviewee in the witness chair would feel less compelled to answer any one of them. Similarly, in a mass communication setting like a radio call-in show, the caller who asks a question and the host or guest who answers it are two halves of a dialectical relationship. The thousands of people who may be listening are observers not participants. If it were possible for all listeners to speak on the air simultaneously, the result would be chaos and there would be no possibility of an interview or any other form of meaningful communication. Interviewing necessarily is dialectical. It requires two parties.

Interviewing is a results oriented communication process. It is an exchange of words performed for the purpose of sending and receiving information. Interviewing is not about the questions; it is about the answers. While interviewers may or may not be skillful in their use of the language, it is almost a requirement that they be nosey. Nosey is a pejorative term, but it is a full and accurate description of one of the qualities of a good interviewer. Many times students in interviewing classes go through the motions of asking questions when they have no interest in the answers. Consequently, they miss the most important information. An interview is not just the asking and answering of questions. Asking and answering questions without motive is equivalent to reading a script or reciting a poem. It has no practical application. A good interview is results oriented; it turns up information or it fails.

Isn't there a social rule about not being nosey? Yes, there is. However, social rules are not a logically worked-out system. They are sometimes contradictory. In this case there is a rule that one should not ask serious questions, and there is also a rule that when asked a serious question one still needs to answer it. The important distinction here for the interviewer is that the rule that compels us to answer tends to override the rule that prohibits the question. Admittedly, this is a barrier for some people. Just as some of us have an overwhelming fear of public speaking, some of us also have a debilitating reluctance to ask tough questions. The solution is the same for both problems. One needs practice and experience to acquire a level of comfort and even confidence. Interviewing exercises that let students script interviews and act them out for interviewing experience miss the point. One can only learn interviewing technique by pushing oneself to ask tough, unanticipated questions with a live interviewee—in other words, by being nosey and getting used to it.

It follows that the interview benefits from spontaneity. Asking predictable questions and getting predictable answers is purely an aesthetic experience. Because interviewing is results oriented, it requires that the interviewer drive the question-asking into deeper and more meaningful territory. The term for this is probing, and it happens in follow-up questioning. An interview or a section of an interview starts with a question that introduces a topic. Topic questions can be written in advance. In a results-oriented interview, however, all of the questions following the topic questions need to be spontaneous. They need to probe the previous answer. Probing is when the interviewer listens to an answer and asks another question that causes the interviewee to go deeper, or at least expand on the answer. If a job applicant says, "I usually got along with my former coworkers," it would be a waste of a good opportunity to change the subject. A better response might be something like, "What do you mean by usually?"

The Rhetorical Situation

The interview can be affected by many things. The interviewer has a great deal of control over some of them and little to no control over others. One of the goals of a professional interviewer is to use everything at his or her disposal to facilitate a successful question and answer process. Question asking is not the only means of manipulating the interview situation. Questions are only part of the rhetorical situation. The rhetorical situation is the physical and psychological environment in which the interview takes place. The main components are the *physical setting*, *social setting*, *perceptions of character*, and *feedback*.

Rhetorical theorist Lloyd Bitzer points out that rhetorical communication does not take place in a vacuum. It is influenced by its environment. In fact Bitzer says that rhetorical communication actually is called for by its environment. Great speeches, lesser speeches, and informal comments are almost always a response to something that preceded them. President

Franklin Roosevelt's famous declaration of war speech where he called December 7 "a date that will live in infamy" was given in response to the bombing of Pearl Harbor. Had the sneak attack on our naval base not occurred, Roosevelt might still have declared war on December 8, but not with this speech, and certainly not with as much rhetorical force. This holds true for informal communication as well. You sit next to someone on a jet. An hour goes by without a word being said. Suddenly there is unexpected turbulence. You comment; the other passenger responds. Why didn't you say anything earlier? There was no need.

In both of the examples above, the ***physical setting*** called for and influenced the communication that followed. The same is true for the ***social setting***. One might feel, for instance, that sitting next to a stranger on a jet requires introductions. Do you feel compelled to say why you are traveling? Should you say what you do for a living? When have you said too much? Is the other party responding? Have you said enough? We read the social environment and determine what and how much to say.

Another influential environmental signpost is the ***character*** of the other person. Whether consciously or unconsciously, we assess those around us, and our observations influence what we say and how we say it. According to Aristotle there are three categories of proofs, that is, three ways to make an argument. They are ethos—character; pathos—emotion; and logos—logic. Aristotle places the most significance on character. He argues that only science and philosophy deal with absolutes. Most of our everyday conversations are about things that range from the unpredictable to the probable. Therefore, he says, our trustworthiness is usually more important than any logical or emotional arguments we can make. Have you ever asked for directions twice because you didn't have confidence in the first person you asked? If you did, whether or not you knew it, you made a character assessment.

Aristotle broke character down into three categories: honesty, knowledge, and goodwill. People spend a great deal of effort trying to impress one another with how smart or knowledgeable they are, but in most cases, it is the least important of the three categories. Goodwill is another face of honesty and trustworthiness. It encompasses kindness, caring, and charity. Goodwill is the opposite of selfishness and maliciousness. Someone with goodwill wants what is best for us and is willing to make small sacrifices for our benefit. If we perceive honesty and goodwill in people, we are comfortable interacting with them; we may even feel obliged to interact with them. The common term for this is rapport.

Goodwill is particularly important in the interview because it is the antidote to probing. Asking tough questions ultimately will alienate an interviewee and result in little information being shared. Goodwill balances the relationship. Tough questions need to be interspersed occasionally with moments when the interviewer expresses kindness and caring. The best interviewers have mastered this technique. Television interviewers like Charlie Rose, Larry King, and Barbra Walters are excellent examples. Expressing goodwill works best for those interviewers who actually feel and relate to the humanity in their interviewees. The object is not to pretend to care, but to find a way to tap the wellspring of compassion that each of us possesses. Watch for the interplay between goodwill and tough probing when you see interviews in the future. Sometimes the two interviewer roles are actually played by two different parties as in what has become known as the "good cop/bad cop scenario."

Feedback refers generally to that part of the rhetorical situation that is created by the interview itself. When interviewees respond to a question with a smile or frown, when they lean forward or pull away from the table, when they raise their voices or whisper, they are changing the rhetorical situation. Good interviewers respond to these influences by adjusting their tone of voice, their expressions, and even by rewording their questions. Feedback tells us when to back off and when to ask the key question.

A more specific use of feedback is for verification. Verification feedback tells us if we understand one another and if our questions are on the right track. It can be obtained through observation or by asking a feedback question. Most of us are experts at recognizing signs of interest, disinterest, understanding, and confusion. If you watch yourself, you will find you change your language sometimes in mid-sentence in response to recognizable feedback: "Oh, dogs! I hate (suddenly the other party stiffens and leans back from the dinner table, a quick glance reveals white dog hairs on the sleeves of her black sweater) . . . people who don't like dogs!" Sometimes we have to ask for clarification, but in either case, there are countless times when proceeding in a dialogue would be hazardous without feedback.

Some police investigators have a vocabulary of signs they look for when asking questions. The signs are called visual accessing codes. The theory holds that when we are remembering and visualizing an actual experience, we tend to look up and to the right. When concocting a fictional experience, we tend to look up and to the left. It is based on the understanding that memory and creative thinking take place in different parts of the brain, and we stimulate or access these areas in part by the way we move our eyes. Of course, this is at best just a tendency, and a skilled interviewee could easily practice and deploy misleading signals.

Types of Interviews

Most people have at least three associations with interviews: journalism, employment, and survey. The journalistic and survey interview represent the first category of interviews called *information gathering*. The focus of the information gathering interview is simply to get information. It is used by not only journalists, but also police, health care professionals, researchers, and anyone who conducts an interview with the primary purpose of collecting data. The survey is unique in that it can take place without the interactive, dynamic presence of the interviewer. The survey process is therefore restricted because it lacks the dimension of spontaneity and it has more limited applications. It does have one advantage over the face-to-face interview interaction, however. Using a survey, it is possible to duplicate the interview experience from interviewee to interviewee, thus providing comparable answers that can be used in mathematical computations.

Employment interviews represent a second category of interview: *observational and accounting*. In the information-gathering interview, the interviewer tries to discover what the interviewee knows about a subject. With the observational and accounting interview, the interviewer attempts to study and probe the behavior and feelings of the interviewee. Regardless of what is being discussed, the interviewee is always the real subject of this interview. The most common application is the employment interview, where the interviewer is trying to discover what the job applicant is really like and predict how he or she will perform as an employee of the company. Counselors, psychologists, and other healthcare professionals use this interview as well, and so do researchers in fields like behavioral sciences and communication.

A third category is the *Socratic method*. The purpose of a Socratic interview is to weigh evidence and reach a logical conclusion. Professors leading classroom discussions often use the Socratic Method. Experienced teachers know that students will remember their lessons better if they arrive at the conclusions in their own way. The goal of the Socratic Method is to teach, but the teacher is really asking questions that help students discover the answers for themselves. This can also be a very effective sales technique. A skillful and patient salesperson with a product or service of actual merit can ask questions that will lead a customer to draw logical conclusions that result in a purchase. What is universally true about the Socratic interview is that the interviewer and interviewee are thinking outloud and moving toward a logical conclusion.

The fourth category is *internal dialogue*. Essentially this means interviewing oneself. Obviously, it would be nonsensical to ask oneself informational questions like "How old are you?" or "Who is your favorite Beatle?" The internal dialogue is essentially the observational and accounting interview or the Socratic method applied internally. Consider that the human brain is like a computer that runs on software. Different software programs cause the central processing unit to process information in different ways. Similarly, the gray matter works best if it is called to action in a meaningful way. Thinking analytically or strategically is most easily and probably most commonly brought about with questions that we pose to ourselves. Think of these questions as creating space and initiating internal processes. "How do I really feel about buying this car . . . taking this job . . . marrying this person?" These initial questions probably turn up several categories of follow-up questions. If one can exhaust the internal dialogue on one of these subjects, one has a wealth of data on which to base an important decision.

It has been argued by rhetorical theorists that learning to develop and give speeches teaches one to think. By studying rhetoric, one not only learns how to become a statesman, but, more importantly, one learns how to become a good citizen. The same can be said for interviewing. The ability to articulate and follow up on meaningful questions with another party hones our skills for articulating and following up on questions within. Analogously, learning to interview is learning to think. The process is essentially the same regardless if the two parties are internal or external. Literature is full of wonderful examples of internal question-asking and answering dialogue. Some notable examples are William Shakespeare's soliloquies in *Hamlet*.

HAMLET:

To be, or not to be: that is the question:
Whether 'tis nobler in the mind to suffer
The slings and arrows of outrageous fortune,
Or to take arms against a sea of troubles,
And by opposing end them? To die: to sleep;
No more; and by a sleep to say we end
The heart-ache and the thousand natural shocks
That flesh is heir to, 'tis a consummation
Devoutly to be wish'd. To die, to sleep;
To sleep: perchance to dream: ay, there's the rub;
For in that sleep of death what dreams may come
When we have shuffled off this mortal coil,
Must give us pause: there's the respect
That makes calamity of so long life;
For who would bear the whips and scorns of time,
The oppressor's wrong, the proud man's contumely,
The pangs of despised love, the law's delay,
The insolence of office and the spurns
That patient merit of the unworthy takes,
When he himself might his quietus make
With a bare bodkin? who would fardels bear,
To grunt and sweat under a weary life,
But that the dread of something after death,
The undiscover'd country from whose bourn

No traveller returns, puzzles the will
And makes us rather bear those ills we have
Than fly to others that we know not of?
Thus conscience does make cowards of us all;
And thus the native hue of resolution
Is sicklied o'er with the pale cast of thought,
And enterprises of great pith and moment
With this regard their currents turn awry,
And lose the name of action.—Soft you now!
The fair Ophelia! Nymph, in thy orisons
Be all my sins remember'd.

Chapter Two

Arrangement

The Guide

Interviewing is both a creative and an analytical process. One needs to be analytical when organizing the interview and creative when writing questions and conducting the interview. It is important to understand this because the mental faculties for creativity and analysis can lead us in very different directions. *Organizing the interview requires reviewing and selecting topics for discussion and ordering them strategically.* Writing and asking questions benefit from a colorful vocabulary and original sentence constructions. Regardless of our strengths, each of us has the capacity to do both, just not at the same time. It is disastrous to write questions without first having created a strategic list of topics. The creative question-writing process may turn up fascinating interrogative sentences, but without the constraints of an analytical framework, the interview will omit key areas of information and be redundant with others. Remember, interviewing is not about the questions; it is about the answers. One must always begin by inventing and arranging topics.

A *list of topics strategically arranged for an interview is called a guide.* The guide has many forms and uses. It might not be written at all. Someone asking questions with a mental agenda is still using a guide. We generate these unwritten guides all the time. If a teenager brings the car home late, he or she faces the universal parenting guide. It looks something like this: discover where the interviewee went, who the interviewee was with, and why the interviewee returned after midnight. Formal interviews like employment or counseling interviews may also occur with just a guide, but the guide is written. A written guide gives the interviewer the advantage of anticipation and makes it easier to follow up on answers or shift focus and still return to the agenda. For instance, if someone says, "I was fired from that job," the interviewer can ask the interviewee to discuss what happened and then pick up the guide again when the line of questioning is exhausted. The guide can also be used as a first step in an interview process that includes writing out the questions in advance. In this case, the guide is developed and then each of the guide items is turned into a question. If the guide item is "employment history," it might be developed into a question that asks, "What was your last job like?"

The two steps to developing a guide are inventing topics to be explored and putting them in the most strategic order. Topics and subtopics for exploration have to be identified before they can be put in order. Because interviewing is a results-oriented process, the invention of topics is governed by an understanding of how the information will be used after the interview is completed. Students often miss this important orientation and conduct interviews as if they were researching encyclopedia articles. Rarely does an interview require discovering everything there is to know about a subject. Good interviews focus on specific information for a specific purpose. The targeted information is then adapted to the area of expertise of the interviewee. If you were a *Rolling Stone* reporter preparing for an interview with Paul McCartney, you might have a guide that included discussing his favorite song, the future of popular music, what he likes to do when he comes to the United States, and how he feels about pirating music. All of these topics fit because they are adapted to his area of expertise, but the answers are not obvious, and they are also areas of interest to *Rolling Stone* readers. They are well arranged because discussing his favorite song is easy and could be fun and will help build rapport. The future of popular music is a logical follow-up topic, and it takes the interview in a more meaningful direction. What he likes to do in the United States is another light, but interesting topic. How he feels about pirating really puts him on the spot because pirating costs him money, but most of his fans do it, and he doesn't want to offend them. It is best placed at the end because the interviewer has developed the most rapport at this point, and the interviewee will feel more compelled to respond.

It was said earlier that even without reading an interviewing book or taking an interviewing class, we are already expert interviewers. This is true even when it comes to developing a guide. We routinely ask ourselves, what do we need to know and what is appropriate to ask? Often we even consider arrangement and decide to start with something that is easy, but not too easy or obvious. When Paul McCartney appeared on *Saturday Night Live*, Chris Farley conducted a mock interview with him. At one point Farley said, "Remember when you were with the Beatles?" The line drew a big laugh. Why? Because we all recognize that the question is profoundly obvious. Farley's bumbling interviewer had the right idea, but extremely poor execution, and everyone knew it.

Invention

Traditionally in the application of rhetoric, invention meant inventing arguments to use in a speech. Invention in interviewing has a different application. Essentially, it means inventing arguments for someone else to use in a speech. In interviewing the listener, or interviewer, is in control of the communication situation and invents topics for the speaker, or interviewee.

The analytical process of inventing topics for the interview begins with *identifying the purpose of the interview*. Police officers interviewing witnesses want to know what happened. Employers interviewing job applicants want to know how they will behave once they are on the job. Consultants interviewing clients want to know what they need. The interview guide is designed not to make the interviewer look good, but to get answers to important questions as efficiently as possible. The interviewer needs to be focused on the anticipated results from the moment he or she begins thinking about the guide until the last question is asked in the interview itself.

Once the purpose of the interview is clear, the interviewer should consider the interviewee. Each interviewee is an expert on something, and a professional interviewer should *identify the interviewee's area of expertise* and not stray outside of it. A campus reporter researching a story on the inadequacy of parking at the university might want to know what it is like trying to find a space, why the parking lot has not been expanded, has a parking garage been considered, what would it cost, and how would it be funded. All of this information cannot be obtained from one source. An interview with a student should focus on the frustration of finding a space. The feasibility and cost of expanding the lot should be discussed with a campus administrator. No one will be interested in a communication student's opinion on what it might cost to build a parking deck, and no one wants to hear about the personal parking experiences of an administrator with a reserved parking space. The student is the expert on the act of parking, and the administrator is the expert on the feasibility of expanding the parking lot. They require very different interviews with different guides.

Students preparing to conduct interviews in class often ask, "What if I get someone who doesn't know anything about my topic?" This isn't really a problem, it is an opportunity. The expertise requirement is not as inhibiting as it might sound. Everyone is an expert at some level. Take recycling, for example. A student conducting an interview on recycling might be assigned an interviewee who recycles, is opposed to recycling, or simply doesn't know anything about it. Each interviewee is an expert. Obviously the interviewee who recycles is an expert on the act of recycling. This interviewee can probably also discuss the practical and philosophical reasons for recycling. Someone who is opposed to recycling is an expert in opposite ways. This interviewee can tell the interviewer what he or she does with waste that is not recycled and why the recycling movement is a distraction or a hoax. What about the person who knows nothing about recycling? He or she may hold the most valuable information of all. The well-prepared interviewer would have guide items that get the uninformed interviewee to discuss public issues of greater importance, sources of information, and experience with waste. The questions might ask: What public issues *are* important to you? What is your main source of news? Have you ever thought about what happens to Styrofoam cups, aluminum cans, or glass bottles? How do you feel when you see cigarette butts on the beach? An environmentalist preparing an awareness campaign would find this information invaluable.

Essentially, if interviewees know a lot about a subject, we want to find out what they know and why they know it. If they know little to nothing about a subject, we want to find out what they don't know and why they don't know it. In business, what people don't know and why they don't know it is usually the most valuable information. I was consulting once for an insurance arbitrator. Each day he visited people whose houses had burned and offered to handle their negotiations with their insurance providers for a fee. He averaged signing up only about a dozen clients a year and was rejected by hundreds. His job was profitable even with the small number of clients, but if he could just sign up one more customer per month he would double his income. A list of research questions was developed for him to ask potential clients, and he was supposed to collect the data for analysis. He called after his first contact and the following conversation ensued.

"Well, what did you find out?"

"Nothing," he said.

"Did you use the interview questions I wrote?"

"No," he said. "She threw me off her property."

"You shouldn't have left so easily. That's the person you most want to interview."

If an interviewer knows the level of expertise of the interviewee before the interview takes place, then the topics can be targeted to the interviewee in advance. If the identity of the interviewee is unknown, then the wise interviewer selects topics over a wide range of expertise.

The list of topics to be discussed in the interview is developed in the cross-section between the purpose of the interview and the area of expertise of the interviewee. A good technique for developing this list is to think about what information you would most like to have when the interview is over. Now, work backwards: what topics need to be covered to get that information? Next, consider the interviewee or potential interviewees. Eliminate the topics that are clearly irrelevant. Don't ask Paul McCartney if he remembers being a Beatle, and don't ask Steven King what kind of novels he writes. Now all you have to do is put the topics in strategic order, and you have a guide. This is all that is needed to conduct an effective interview. If the situation requires it, the guide can be turned into a schedule of questions by writing one question for each guide item.

When the identity of the interviewee is uncertain, it may be useful to develop two or three sets of guide items or even questions. A sports reporter preparing an interview with a professional baseball player is so aware of what he or she wants to know and so aware of the level of expertise of the interviewee that the guide might direct the interviewee to discuss specific pitches. But the same reporter interviewing a fan after the game has no idea of the level of focus or expertise of the interviewee. The guide for a successful interview with the player might have only five items. The guide for the random fan should have more like fifteen: five if the fan followed the game closely, five if the fan is a casual follower of baseball, and five if the fan isn't really a fan at all and attended the game for some other reason. These interviews directed toward different interviewees might result in asking the ballplayer, "Do you think you might have caught that foul pop-up if the fan hadn't interfered?" asking the dedicated fan why the team hasn't won a pennant since 1945, asking the casual fan to compare the playoff atmosphere to the regular season, and asking the tourist how he or she liked Wrigley Field.

Arrangement

While interviewing has much in common with speech-making and writing, it is also significantly different because it is a true dialogue. That is, the interview is not just about the information that is exchanged, it is also about the two people who are exchanging that information. It is not enough to simply come up with a list of topics and expect the interviewee to address fully each one of them. Consider all the human factors that might prevent an interviewee from answering a simple question like "Why did you decide to go to college at Purdue?" The interviewee might not remember. The interviewee might give an answer that is misleading or make something up. The interviewee might misunderstand the question and discuss reasons for just attending college. Or, the interviewee might feel the interviewer is prying into a private matter and not want to answer at all.

No, the interviewer does not have the control of a writer or speechmaker and cannot afford to focus only on the topic. The interviewer must take the interviewee into account in ways that go far beyond the accommodations typically made for readers or audiences. ***Interviewing necessarily attends to the logical and psychological dimensions of the relationship.***

There are two categories of concern regarding the interviewee: one, motivating the interviewee to participate, and, two, helping the interviewee process information as efficiently as possible. Both concerns are addressed through arrangement. Arrangement deals with motivation in the interview by creating a rhythm that begins with easy, enjoyable conversation and moves toward more difficult and even stressful questions and answers. This rhythm or cycle applies to the interview as a whole and also to sections of the interview. It is useful to begin the interview with a topic that the interviewee is most interested in. It is difficult if not impossible to motivate someone artificially. A wise interviewer will tap into the reservoir of motivation that the interviewee already possesses. As the interview progresses, the interviewer and interviewee become more familiar with one another and, hopefully, develop a level of trust and mutual concern. This buildup of trust isn't so much a tactical exercise as it is a normal bonding that takes place whenever two people talk and share things about themselves. The longer the interview goes on, the greater potential for developing trust and mutual concern and the more likely the interviewee is to attempt to answer difficult questions. Logically, we place the most difficult topics in the middle or at the end of the interview. This arrangement strategy is routinely used in surveys, which save the sometimes highly personal demographic topics like age and income for the very end. This rhythm is also the pattern under each topic, the first questions introducing the topic, and each question thereafter probing into deeper sometimes more guarded territory.

One simple rule to follow regarding motivation in interviews is to respect the interviewee. Never assume that you are cleverer than the interviewee. Some clumsy, often detrimental things have been said by interviewers in a misguided attempt to motivate interviewees. One of the worst tactics is to make small talk at the beginning of the interview. An interviewer needs to be taken seriously and to have the trust of the interviewee. Telling a joke or discussing an uneventful day of weather will have the opposite effect. In the classroom, it tends to signal to the interviewee that it is ok to make up answers, which makes probing impossible. A good place to start an interview is on a topic of mutual interest.

For most of us, motivation steps come naturally; helping the interviewee process information requires more strategy and a basic understanding of cognition. Cognition means thinking, and researchers who study cognition believe that our brains store and access information somewhat in the manner of squirrels storing and accessing acorns. The process seems random, yet the squirrel finds its acorns and survives the winter. No one knows for sure how squirrels do this, and no one can say for sure how you remember the color of your first bicycle or what you had for lunch yesterday, but we have theories that partially explain these things. Theories on cognition can be helpful in interviewing because every time we ask someone to answer a factual question, we are asking them to remember something.

The most useful theory of cognition for the interviewer deals with information processing. Information processing theory holds that information is linked, and that when we think of one thing, it stimulates us to think about other things that are related to it—other things that we might not have remembered if we had not thought of the more familiar memory first. For instance, your first bicycle, if you think about it do you also remember the sidewalk or the street you rode on? The information processing theory of cognition holds that if we follow these memories, more and more will come back to us. Now, since the internal and external interview are essentially the same process, doesn't it make sense for the interviewer to structure the interview in a way that helps the interviewee remember?

Introduction

It is helpful to think of the similarities between interior space and exterior space. The analogous relationship between interior space and exterior space goes back at least as far as classical Greece and is still with us today. Comments like "Where are you going with this" or "Don't go there" clearly overlay the exterior and interior landscapes. With this in mind, think of the interview as a journey. The interviewer and interviewee are going to go for a walk through the interviewee's interior space. What do we do first when we walk? We identify our destination and we pick a route. The same should be done at the beginning of the interview. Tell the interviewee what you want to talk about and ask a first question that will begin the process, thus one moves from familiar territory to less familiar territory. An interview is not organized like an essay or a news story. An interviewer intending to write a story based on the interview will reorganize the data. The interview begins and develops conforming to the interior landscape of the interviewee. An interviewer who anticipates and follows the interviewee's internal pathways will get more information than the interviewer who violates them.

The study of rhetoric suggests several options for introductions: introduction inquisitive, introduction paradoxical, introduction corrective, introduction preparatory, and introduction narrative. Each has the potential to signal where the interview is headed and to motivate the interviewee to proceed. *Introduction inquisitive characterizes the topic as interesting or perhaps newsworthy.* Using this approach, an interview with Bob Dylan might begin with "You once wrote 'Ah, but I was so much older then, I'm younger than that now.' How do you feel about that now that you are over 60?" *Introduction paradoxical signals that the subject is not what it seems.* One might begin an interview with basketball coach Phil Jackson by asking, "How does a student of meditative Eastern religions find happiness coaching in one of the most fast-paced, frenetic sports on the planet?" It is apparent the interview will have two subjects and that incongruity will be its theme. *Introduction corrective addresses a misreported fact or mistaken notion.* One might ask a college student who was home-schooled, "One of the arguments against home schooling is that it doesn't allow for the development of social skills; what do you think about that?" *Introduction preparatory lets the interviewee know that the interview will take an unexpected or unusual direction.* An employment interview for an alcoholism counselor might begin with "Normally job interviewers don't probe into people's private lives, but because this is a rehab counseling position, I need to know, what are your experiences with alcohol abuse?" *Introduction narrative indicates the interview will be comprised of storytelling.* This not only signals the subject of the interview, but also its form, as storytelling is composed of chronological, uninterrupted, detailed narratives. It might begin with a demonstration: "I talked to a veteran once who said his most vivid memory of D-Day was the smell of dead fish. What can you share with me about your experience?" The words "what can you share" also imply that the interviewer will be cautious.

It is useful if the interviewer can motivate the interviewee to participate fully. As mentioned above, picking a subject of mutual interest serves this purpose. Another important step is making the ethical appeal. In speechmaking it is believed that the speaker must indicate he or she is worthy of the audience's attention with an ethical appeal. *The ethical appeal is divided into three categories: honesty, goodwill, and knowledge.* If you are giving a speech, your audience is more likely to listen and act on your words if they believe you speak the truth, have their best interests in mind, and if you know more about the topic than they do. The same is true for the interviewer, only in the interview, the ethical appeal is even more important. In a speech, the other parties are passive, they merely listen to a speaker. In an interview, the interviewer is really the audience, the interviewee is the speaker. We might listen to a speech out of politeness, but talking about and revealing our deepest thoughts requires motivation and trust. Since the interviewer is usually a stranger to the interviewee, developing this trust quickly and early in the interview is essential.

Unfortunately, there is no universal tactic for making the ethical appeal in the introduction of an interview. Each interviewer has a unique value system and has acquired knowledge unique to his or her experience. Furthermore, it is considered impolite to announce abruptly that you are honest, well meaning, and smart. Such an outburst would have the antithesis of the intended effect. It is best if the interviewer knows of the need for the ethical appeal and looks for opportunities to make it with subtlety. A journalist makes the appeal simply by saying, "I am a reporter for . . ." In this case, the reputation of the profession and of the particular publication makes the ethical appeal. Business cards or framed diplomas on our walls showing initials like M.S., M.D., or Ph.D. speak for us about our knowledge and professionalism. There can even be an element of the ethical appeal in the way we dress, shake hands, or smile. Rather than insert an awkward sentence that might seem like bragging, it is best for the interviewer to understand the necessity of the ethical appeal and look for opportunities to inject it smoothly and spontaneously into the interview in its early development. For instance, a doctor might say, "I have seen three other cases like this . . ." Or a software troubleshooter might say, "they sent me over because I helped write this program." However, keep in mind, the interview is about the interviewee, not the interviewer. Develop the ethical appeal early and then drop it. Interviewers who spend the entire interview looking for opportunities to talk about themselves are wasting time and probably not paying close enough attention to their interviewees.

Body

The body of the interview follows the interview guide. Guide items should be a few words that suggest the topic. They are not questions. Think of the guide as a list of places you wish to visit during the interview. The best way to develop a guide is to write it down. Once your ideas are in front of you, sort them out. Make sure you have listed all the important points. Eliminate the redundant topics, and add the missing ones. Spontaneous topic selection or random lists of topics rarely produce a good interview. Developing a guide is the best way to insure a productive interview.

When developing the guide, it is useful to consider what kinds of questions might be pursued following the guide item. However, in most cases, it is counterproductive to write these questions down. The questions following the guide items need to be based on the interviewee's answer, and if the questions are worthy, there is no way to predict what those answers will be. If the interviewer could predict the answer, there would be no point in asking the question.

An interview that uses only a guide is called a moderately scheduled interview. Most journalistic and employment interviews are moderately scheduled. This open structure allows for the greatest opportunity to discover new information. However, when the interviewer already knows the probable answers, a requirement for most surveys, the interview can be used not to discover information, but to confirm it. In this case most or all of the questions are written in advance. When all the questions are written in advance of the actual interview and the interviewer merely records answers, the interview is called highly scheduled. In most survey interviews the answer options are also pre-written. This further facilitates speedy quantification of preconceived answers, and it is called a highly scheduled standardized interview.

Writing questions is the creative part of the interview preparation process. Developing the guide is analytical: one asks oneself, "What do I want to know?" In the creative questions-writing part of the process, one asks instead, "How can I find this out? The question-asking tactics include style and vocabulary choices and in some cases even practicing delivery.

All interviews have schedules. Interviews, by definition, require that the interviewer have a preconceived objective. Whatever form the objective or objectives take, whether they are written or unwritten, they function as a rough guide.

Conclusion

There is no practical reason for a conclusion unless the interviewer plans to interview the interviewee again. However, there are pressing social and psychological needs for leave-taking, and a professional interviewer should attend to them. Interviews can sometimes be intense intellectual and emotional experiences. It is good not to end them suddenly. A way to ease into the end of the interview is to signal the interview is almost over by say something like, "My last question is about . . ." Next, anyone who takes the time to answer our questions needs to be thanked. Like the interview itself, this is best if it is not scripted. The interviewer should simply thank the interviewee in his or her own words when the moment presents itself. In most cases it is also good to tell the interviewee what you learned in a broad general way: "I have read many stories about the New Orleans hurricane of 2005, but yours is the first personal account I have heard. Thank you for taking the time . . ."

Chapter Three

Questions

Rhetoric and Power

Perhaps you have heard the expression, "Sticks and stones may break my bones, but words will never hurt me." Parents and teachers pass this old maxim on to children to help them get through the trauma of name-calling and other acts of verbal bullying. While it may be helpful to believe that words cannot hurt us as children, as adults we need to understand that speaking words is a significant exercise of power. Words are not harmless: they shape reality, they direct action, they can soothe our pain, and they can, indeed, hurt us.

Simply put, what we say affects what others say and do around us. This is why rhetoric has been studied and taught in Western cultures for over 2,000 years. Unlike the study of communication or language, rhetoric is concerned with effect. The art of rhetoric is the ethical use of communication as an exercise of power. The use of communication to exercise power without ethical constraints is merely persuasion.

Historically we have thought of rhetoric and power in terms of things like giving a speech to rally troops for battle, pass legislation, or mount a defense in a courtroom. However, this traditional focus overlooks the area where words have their greatest impact—the rhetoric of interpersonal communication. An interpersonal rhetoric book, if it existed, might discuss the strategies and tactics of expressing and rejecting love, the canons of good leadership, and the pitfalls of dishonesty. Great speeches get the most attention, but their impact is far outweighed by the cumulative effect of words that pass between mothers and children or brothers in arms.

Children discover the power of words for themselves in spite of well-meaning, misleading maxims from adults. They learn the power of question asking almost as soon as children learn to speak. Have you ever heard a child in what could be called the "why phase"? It might have sounded like this:

Parent: It's time for bed.

Child: Why?

Parent: Because you need sleep.

Child: Why?

Parent: I don't know, so you won't suffer from sleep deprivation, I guess.

Child: Why?

Parent: To keep the neurons in your brain from malfunctioning!

Child: Why?

Two things are curious about conversations like this. One is that the child is motivated to keep asking why even though he or she has no real interest in the answers, and the other is that the adult keeps answering the questions even though it is apparent the child has no interest in the answers.

The child's motivation is easy to understand if the situation is looked at from the child's point of view. After a year or two of being placed in and out of car seats, told when to eat and sleep, a child works the word why into a crude sentence and suddenly the action stops and one of the large unpredictable creatures in the room is looking down and speaking. As long as the child says the word why, the adult stays glued to the situation. Other than crying, it is the child's first exercise of power over the outside world.

Social Rules

An explanation for the adults' actions can be found in what social scientists call rules theory. Rules theorists contend that everyday life is infinitely complicated and that if we had to weigh intellectually every choice we made, we would never be able to navigate through the day. They believe that we learn patterns of behavior and that we follow them without thinking about them. At the physical level we learn routines like walking and eating, and at the social level we learn patterns of behavior that allow us to speak and interact with others. These things we do automatically without having to consider "How far should I bend my knee when I take this next step?" or "I wonder what will happen if I put my waste basket over my head and walk around the office." Instead, we reserve our conscious thought processes for more sophisticated issues like deciding whether or not to run for the bus or if it is a good day to ask for a raise.

The patterns of social behavior are governed by tacit rules. Tacit rules are social guidelines to which we adhere but about which we do not talk. Like most of what we study in the social sciences, these rules cannot be proven with the certainty in which we know the atomic weight of gold or the temperature at which water freezes. That is probably why they are called rules instead of laws. They are observations with great explanatory power.

There are two rules hypotheses that are especially useful for interviewing. One is a tacit rule that it is almost always permissible to ask a question. The other is that questions must be answered. This means that in most situations people adhere to social rules that mandate they let themselves be interrupted for questions and that when questions are asked, they must answer them. This doesn't mean that all people behave in a completely predictable manner, but that most of the time they will follow these social rules without thinking, and that if they contemplate not following them, they will feel a degree of social or psychological pressure.

Interpersonal vs. Public Rhetoric

The social question-asking, question-answering mechanism provides an arena where rhetoric can be used to exercise a power not accounted for by classical theorists who were mainly focused on public speaking—that is on communicating with audiences of two or more. Rhetorical studies account for questions in speeches, but question-asking is significantly different when the question is addressed to more than one person. Consider the difference between a teacher asking the class, "What do we mean by explanatory power?" and a teacher calling on you by name and saying, "define explanatory power for me." In the study of speechmaking a question to the audience is called a rhetorical question, the implication being that it is done for artistic effect and that the speaker does not expect an answer. This is decidedly not the case in a one-on-one verbal interaction. If you ask someone a question, look him or her in the eye, and wait for an answer, you will get one. We can say, then, that while interviewing may put to use all the strategies and tactics of the rhetorical arts, it may also apply them for an effect that is not accessible in any other communicative venue.

It is important that anyone who wishes to study or make use of interviewing theory understand this power distinction. The power of question asking is the defining characteristic of the interview. Plato whimsically compares the study of rhetoric to the study of boxing in "The Gorgias." But the analogy is much more substantial when one considers the rhetoric of interpersonal communication. Granted, no blows are exchanged. Boxing is physical where interviewing is intellectual, but both are exercises of the strategic use of force. Anyone who doubts this need only look at news stories that freed inmates on death row or brought down political regimes. Republican apologists for Richard Nixon might blame his demise on FBI official Mark Felt for blowing the whistle, but a more objective analysis would have to give a great deal of credit to the interviewing skills of *Washington Post* reporters Bob Woodward and Carl Bernstein who unraveled the story of the Watergate break-in and cover-up.

Garfinkeling

The best way to appreciate the power of question-asking is to experience it for yourself. The study of implied social rules is called ethnomethodology. Sociologist Harold Garfinkel developed a way of testing if social rules exist or not, and it can be applied by anyone at any time. He suggests testing rules by violating them. If you hypothesize that a common sense, unspoken social rule exists, then break it and see what happens. Garfinkeling, as it is sometimes called, can easily be used to test social rules regarding question-asking and answering. You can test whether or not there is a social rule about having to answer questions by not answering them. Wait for someone to ask you for the time, or how your day has gone, or for your opinion, and don't respond. Unless you are a sociopath, you should feel mounting pressure, and both parties will show discomfort. In all likelihood, you will be unable to complete the experiment. Test another rule by Garfinkeling in reverse. Pick a moment in a conversation where it seems inappropriate to interrupt someone and interrupt him or her with a question. If the speaker stops and responds, the implication is that the rule allowing questions overrides the rule about not interrupting someone.

This informal application of Garfinkeling is suggested only to make the power of interviewing more tangible. Real social scientists have a much more rigorous procedure for testing rules, and they would admit that their findings are ultimately only probabilities of human behavior, not absolute laws of science. However, even informal Garfinkeling should be performed responsibly. One Purdue student hypothesized that there is a social rule governing highway lane usage. Her theory held that if you pass someone up, there is a social rule that requires that you drive faster than the person you just passed. To test this, she passed cars on Indiana's Borman Expressway, cut in front of them, and then slowed down. Needless to say, the other drivers helped her prove her theory with certain highway gesturing rituals punctuated by horn blowing and swift acceleration. The last driver she tested tried to run her off the road.

Exigence and Stasis

Something that creates psychological pressure requiring us to respond is called an *exigence*. An exigence can effect an entire population or it can be personal; it can come out of the environment or it can be the result of human communication. The Challenger disaster and the Iran Contra scandal were national exigencies, which called for and received fitting public speeches from President Ronald Reagan. Exigence can also occur in powerful ways on the interpersonal level. If you miss an important meeting, for example, you feel an exigence to explain your absence. All exigencies are not the result of events beyond our control, however. We create exigence every time we ask a question. Because there are social rules allowing for questions and requiring that they be answered, we create and dissolve exigence in everyday conversation with questions and answers.

Stasis is a concept we all understand, but you probably didn't know there was a word for it. Stasis refers to the point at which an argument rests. If you have ever said, "what are you getting at," or "what I mean is this," you were referring to stasis. What was the stasis point in the international debate over the invasion of Iraq? Everyone knows it had to do with what the government called weapons of mass destruction. The United Nations said there were none, and the U.S. government said it had reliable reports that they existed. Stasis is usually not the only item being discussed or debated; it is the underlying issue to which all the other topics relate.

There are many things to learn about the art of interviewing, but the key skill is this: find the stasis point of the discussion and create an exigence for it. If you are buying a sports car in Minnesota and the seller says, "It runs great in warm weather," the best follow up question is not "How fast does it go?" The question that places the exigence on the stasis point is: "What happens when it gets cold?"

Open and Closed Questions

Generally speaking, the best information is the hardest to come by. Journalists understand that if everyone knows something, then it isn't news. Counselors understand that if the patient knew the answers he or she probably wouldn't be a patient. Interviewing techniques are applied when we need to obtain information that is not apparent and not volunteered. It is almost axiomatic, then, that one or two questions are not going to reveal the information we seek. We have to work for it. To a great extent, the value of the information is proportional to the effort it takes to acquire it. Productive interviews are not made up of independent questions; they are questions in sequence that drive the interviewee deeper into faded memories and emotional shadows.

If we know that one or two questions will not produce information of value, then an important skill for an interviewer is the ability to keep the discussion alive. This is accomplished mainly with the use of one simple tactic—the open question. An open question is one that implies little or nothing about the possible answer. The opposite is a closed question, which clearly has limited answers. Closed questions can ask for a yes or no response, or they can be multiple choice. Open questions have infinite answer options. Obviously, closed questions have less potential to produce information, but they also present a procedural problem. A closed question is detrimental to an interview because it brings closure to the topic. Logically and emotionally, closed questions do not open up, they conclude: "So did you switch universities to be closer to home?" The interviewer can next ask the interviewee to compare campuses, to discuss home life, or to evaluate the school football team, but probing deeper into the reason for dropping out of one school and enrolling in another is, for all practical purposes, off limits. Now consider the options for probing if the question had been open, for instance: "So you switched universities after your junior year; how did you reach that decision?" This question propels the interview deeper. The interviewee says, "I realized I wanted to be a writer, and I needed to be in a creative writing program." The interviewer follows up with another open question: "What made you realize you wanted to write?" The interviewee says, "Mostly I was inspired by Jack Kerouac." The interviewer asks, "Why Jack Kerouac?" Open questions keep the probing sequence alive and almost invariably drive it deeper.

Asking open questions sounds easy, but it is quite difficult for most of us. This is probably because it feels like we are giving control of the interview over to the interviewee. We intuitively limit the answer options to maintain our authority. It is a bad habit. The best way for the interviewer to control the interview is by causing the interviewee to remember and confess information that was previously unknown. It is self-defeating to steer the interview into familiar and predictable territory. The effect of letting go and using open questions is quite profound. Student interviewers often stumble into deep meaningful discussions without having exercised any degree of control or direction other than staying on topic and keeping their questions open.

Closed questions have their uses. Sometimes it is necessary to bring closure to a topic. Asking a closed question is an effective and subtle precursor to shifting subjects: "So, do you like the writing program at Columbia College?" Sometimes closed questions are needed to clarify or confirm information. If a job applicant says, "My cash drawer came up short occasionally," the job interviewer probably needs to ask how often is "occasionally?" Closed questions can also help get an interview started if it is stalled. They are easier to ask, and they are easier to answer as well. The most important thing to understand about closed and open questions is that open questions are the rule and closed questions are the exception. We should be asking open questions by force of habit, and closed questions only when they are necessary.

Open questions can be categorized by their degree of openness. The most open question is the silent probe. A silent probe is exercised by simply not asking a question when there is an expectation that one will be asked. This breaking of the question-answer pattern creates a tremendous exigence. It would be hard for an interviewee not to conclude that there is a problem with the previous answer. In order to make the exigence go away, the interviewee will search for and volunteer more information, all of it gravitating deeper into the stasis point. Unfortunately the interviewer feels just as much anxiety over the exigence as the interviewee. Not responding to an interviewee's answer, after all, breaks a social rule that says if you ask a question, and someone answers it, you need to express interest and or approval. This makes the non-question the most difficult question to ask. Often an interviewer will break the silence before the interviewee can answer.

The Probing Sequence

Open topic questions are used at the beginning of a probing sequence to introduce a subject and its parameters. The question, "What do you know about the polar ice caps?" introduces a topic and is open, but it sets no direction for the interview. The interviewee could talk about history, geography, ecology, politics, or economics. If the interview is supposed to be about the effects of global warming, then a better open topic question might be: "What do you know about the shrinking of the polar ice caps?" This question is still quite open, but it avoids wasting time shifting the interviewee from discussing 19th century polar exploration to 21st century global politics.

Follow-up probing questions are increasingly more focused, yet still open. Let's say the interviewee's answer to the topic question is "My research shows that the Arctic ice cap is at the smallest size ever recorded." Keeping the questions open, but continuing to focus, the interviewer might ask, "What kind of evidence do you have?" The interviewee might respond, "Well, the storied Northwest Passage may be opening up, allowing ships to sail from western Europe to the western United States without having to go through the Panama Canal."

Once the sequence has run its course, the interviewer may want to ask the topic question again, but without the parameters: "So, what else do you know about the polar ice caps?" The interviewee may have some relevant observations that the interview did not discover, and this will flush them out. If, however, the interviewee raises a nonrelevant issue, the interviewer can close the line of questioning and move on without having encumbered the development of the interview. This topic-only question is sometimes called a clearing-house probe.

The end of a sequence is also a reasonable place to ask a necessary closed question. Typically this will be a comprehension question. In other words, if the interviewee has provided a great deal of detail, the interviewer may want to try to put it together by asking something like, "So, you are saying global temperatures are steadily rising and melting the ice caps, and this actually may have some benefits for the shipping industry, including replacing the trip around Panama with one across northern Canada that will take about one third the amount of time?" This serves several functions: it wraps up part of the discussion, it allows the interviewer to make sure he or she got the information correctly, and it tells the interviewee the interviewer has been listening. This last point is an important one, since most of us are such poor listeners. An expert on a topic may have had several bad experiences discussing his or her field. When an interviewer provides evidence of comprehension, it can create considerable motivation for the interviewee to continue the interview process.

Neutral and Leading Questions

Another important tactic that may take some practice is asking neutral as opposed to leading questions. A neutral question is rhetorically inactive; a leading question creates a rhetorical vacuum. A neutral question betrays none of the preferences or expectations of the interviewer. A leading question does the opposite; it makes it emotionally or logically easier to answer one way rather than another. Leading questions can be overt: "Don't you think football is boring?" or they can be subtle, "Do you approve of violent sports like football?" The first question supplies the answer and it creates psychological pressure by using the emotionally charged word "boring." The second question is more insidious. "Do you approve" seems to bias the question in the affirmative, but the words "approve" and "violent" have negative connotations. We usually only use the word "approve" in conjunction with issues that are questionable enough to require approval. In other words, one might reasonably ask, "Do you approve of gambling," but it would be syntactically illogical to ask, "Do you approve of baseball?" Furthermore, the word "violent" is clearly pejorative. The combination of "approve" and "violent" in conjunction with "football" implies that the interviewer expects the interviewee to answer no—to agree with the interviewer.

Does an interviewee have to succumb to the pressure of an interviewer asking a leading question? Of course not. We are all familiar with leading questions, and there are times when we have ignored or contradicted them. In fact, some interviewees may even go out of their way to contradict what they perceive are the expectations of an interviewer. Still, the predominant tendency on the part of most people is to go with the prevailing opinion. Typically, if an interviewer lets his or her opinion leak into the dialogue, the interviewee will provide an answer that either is in agreement with, or is modified by, the perceived interviewer opinion. The result is an answer that reflects the process more than the subject; it is bad data.

Practice

Much of what we learn about rhetoric and communication needs to be internalized. That is, we learn it, we practice it, then we don't think about it anymore. It becomes incorporated in the way we interact with others by force of habit. This is the case with open and closed, and neutral and leading questions. A good way to learn them is to practice asking only closed questions, then practice asking only open questions. This will make you more aware of the distinction. Pick a topic, say gun control, and interview someone using only closed questions: "Do you own a gun?" "How long have you owned it?" "Do you think we need stricter controls on handgun ownership?" The interview will be over quickly, because there is little or no opportunity for follow-up questions. Now practice on someone with only open questions: "Tell me about your personal experience with handguns?" Follow up with open probing questions, then go to the next open primary question: "How do you feel about the National Rifle Association?" More open follow-up, then: "What would you do if someone broke into your house?" Once the distinction becomes intuitive, practice asking the open questions in longer sequences. Now, do the same with leading and neutral questions. Remember, it may be necessary to ask closed or even leading questions during the course of an interview, but they need to be asked on purpose, not by accident.

Probing

Conducting an interview is analogous to looking up a word in a dictionary. Let's say you want a definition of the word byte. First you open the dictionary, parting the pages close to the front cover. You look at the top of the page. You are in the Cs, so you page back to the Bs. You see the word Beach in the upper margin, and you flip pages until you see Byzantine. Now you look down the edge of the page for byt: Byronic, bystander, byte. Having found the definition, you read it: A group of eight binary digits used in computing.

Finding words in a dictionary and retrieving information from human experience are both processes. Take a simple interviewing task like asking a witness for a description of a bank robber. Remembering details about size, weight, dress, and mannerisms comes easy for some people, but most of us would have trouble focusing on trivial details if someone had just pointed a gun in our direction. A professional interviewer might start with "How did you first become aware of the robbery?" The witness might say: "Someone cut in the front of the line to see the teller, and he looked suspicious." The interviewer would ask, "What was suspicious about him?" The witness mentions a high collar, floppy hat, and sunglasses. The interviewer asks about the rest of his clothes, and the witness says, "I couldn't see them." The interviewer asks why. The witness says because he was shorter than the other people in the line. In this manner the interview proceeds through the memories of the interviewee, paging to the needed information. The interviewer's process parallels and aids the interviewee's internal process. Together they look up memories and impressions. Police who do not understand that this is a process might start with "What did he look like?" and get an incomplete or misleading answer. Then, perhaps hours or days later, the witness might call the police station and say, "I have been thinking about the robbery at the bank, and I remembered that . . ." What happened is that as time passed the witness began to reflect on the incident and more information came to mind. A great deal of time could have been saved if the original interviewer had been more patient and methodical with the first interview.

Of course, probing through someone else's brain is a lot more difficult than looking up words in a dictionary. You can't say, "Think about 2005, now think about October, now find October 6, and tell me what you had for breakfast." Each interviewee has multiple methods for filing and retrieving information and interviewing is necessarily an adaptive, creative process. While the interview process is governed by the interviewer, the structure for the interview is best determined by the interviewee. The interviewer might not even perceive a logical relationship between the answers. A probing sequence begins with an open primary question, and it proceeds by focusing on the stasis point in each answer and creating exigence with the next open question. When the interview is over, it may be apparent that the questions and answers were chronological, or that they followed a cause and effect progression, or that there was no logical relationship between the answers. Structure in interviewing is not like structure in speeches and essays. In a probing interview, structure is incidental to the process and should not be predetermined.

Maintaining Control of the Interview

The object in interviewing is not to control the message, it is to control the flow of the message. This is accomplished in part by not asking questions that allow the interviewee to shift focus. Journalists often complain about slippery politicians, but often the journalists are the ones lubricating the interview when they use double-barreled questions. A double-barreled question is really two or more questions asked at once. Journalists frequently ask double-barreled questions in press conferences, and it is easy to see why. If a reporter realizes he or she may only get one chance to ask a question, it is tempting to string two or three together. A smart interviewee will pick the easiest question, answer that, and then call on another reporter.

An entire category of problematic questions are those that close off or allow the interviewee to close off an avenue of inquiry. Mostly they are various types of closed questions. Sometimes closed questions are useful or even necessary; it is the accidental closed questions that interviewers need to avoid. An accidental closed question asks, "Do you like the new Clint Eastwood movie?" when it should ask, "What do you think of the new Clint Eastwood movie?" Open questions usually put an interviewee on the spot more than closed questions, and interviewers feel that psychological pressure as well. That is probably why we all have a tendency to ask closed questions. This explains an odd but fairly common interviewing phenomenon of asking an open question at the beginning of the sentence, and then converting it to a closed question at the end of the sentence. For instance, "What do you think of *Million Dollar Baby*; would you see it again?" The first half of the question opens doors to talk about plot, acting, directing, cinematography, whatever is of most interest to the interviewee. The second half of the question is limited to yes or no. If the interviewee responds with "Yes!", then the interviewer has to start over by asking, "What did you like about it?" If the interviewee answers "No.", then the line of questioning is truncated.

Leading questions also close off lines of development. If the interviewer accidentally allows his or her opinion to leak into the question it will color the answer, usually by causing the interviewee to agree or avoid confrontation by being neutral. In either case, the potential for probing the thoughts of the interviewee has been restricted. Common sense tells us if we want to find out if someone smoked marijuana, we shouldn't start the sequence with "I think marijuana smoking is a disgusting habit; how do you feel about it?" This is an obvious leading question—the interviewer clearly stated an opinion.

Subtle leading questions are a greater concern because the interviewer may be unaware he or she is using them. An interviewer doing research on the cultural impact of a new casino might start with "How do you think legalized gambling has affected the community?" Without intending to, the interviewer has reminded the interviewee that gambling used to be illegal, and that not everyone supports it—all because the word "legalized" was used. Also the word "gambling" is slightly problematic. It carries a history of negative connotations. That is why casinos refer to themselves as being in the "gaming" industry.

Some leading question wording is almost unavoidable. An interviewer researching alcohol consumption and motor vehicle usage would be hard pressed not to use the words "drunk" and "driving." Yet, asking someone "Do you drink and drive?" is about the same as saying "Are you a drunk driver?" People at bars or private parties don't say to one another, "I think I will drink and drive tonight." That is the language of Alcoholics Anonymous and Mothers Against Drunk Driving. This topic requires slow, open, neutral development. A good first question might be "What did you do to celebrate your 21st birthday?"

Chapter Four

Listening: Interviewing's Fourth Canon

Interviewing is the counterpart of speechmaking; it focuses on receiving a message rather than sending one. While the speaker might strategize how best to be heard—delivery, the interviewer strategizes how best to hear—listening. Just as there is more to delivery than simply opening one's mouth and talking, there is more to listening than merely hearing what someone says. Listening is a mental discipline with strategies and tactics that benefits from training and practice.

Communication Skills

Other than reading, most of what we think of as communication skills are really thinking skills. When we learn to read, we assume the writer's ideas have already been considered and articulated; we mainly decode them. This is not the case with speaking, writing, and listening, where our reasoning capabilities play a large role. In courses dealing with speech and writing, we learn to select topics, generate ideas, organize our thoughts, and apply reason to develop logical conclusions. Therefore, learning to give speeches and write essays is really learning to think. The communication skills portion of these subjects is a small pool of information dealing with vocalizing and drawing symbols that translate our thoughts for others.

Learning to Listen and Listening to Learn

Listening really is in a category by itself. At one level, we could say it is parallel to reading. Someone else has done all the thinking for us; we merely are decoding the information; the only difference between listening and reading is the medium. However, this is not the case. Listening is the precursor to all of the other communication skills and to reasoning itself. Children learn to speak and reason by listening to others. No matter how much effort parents and teachers make to pass on mental habits and knowledge, the learning process must begin unaided in the netherworld of infant consciousness, where sounds take on meaning and we begin to construct information processes.

We have the ability to listen at birth, and it is nurtured and developed every conscious moment of our lives. Claiming to teach a lesson on listening is almost ludicrous. Anyone who attends class or reads the homework already has developed a listening apparatus that is infinitely more sophisticated than any lecture, book, or computer model could hope to emulate. Reading, writing, and public speaking are more easily taught because they are learned and practiced with commonly understood symbols and behaviors. To some extent this is also true with listening when it can be qualified outwardly with concepts like comprehension and accuracy, but the true listening construct bridges back to the larger, murkier domain of precognitive consciousness. Here listening behavior emerges from wisps of inherited and biological tendencies like curiosity, sensitivity to feedback, and the joy of comprehension. Much of our listening development already has to have taken place before we can begin to learn about the other communication skills.

Regrettably there is no way to grow good listening behavior by implanting precognitive listening threads. However, it might be possible for us to discover our own deepest motivations for listening. Are you curious or nosey, do you value learning, are you contemplating a theory of behavior or culture? Is life more meaningful, more real, when people speak what is on their minds and do not mince words? Try thinking of who you are in terms of what you want to know. If you take the time to better understand how and why you listen, it becomes possible to nurture these interests and tendencies and transform them into a self-motivated personal listening process.

Self-motivation is the most powerful listening aid, but to a great extent self-motivational strategies are different for each of us. They must be discovered and implemented by the individual. Unfortunately students often select self-motivational strategies that are counterproductive for listening and learning. Goals like getting a degree so that I can get a job, or proving that I can get an A, have no connection to the cognitive process of learning; in fact, they are almost anti-intellectual. Students who learn best are interested in learning for learning's sake. It is the same with listening— probably because listening and learning are almost synonymous. The journalist who is most interested in the story will likely come away from the interview with the best information, and the employment interviewer with the most interest in human nature will probably have picked up the most meaningful information from the job candidate. Discover what you want to know, and you will discover how to listen.

Listening Comprehension

Those of us in communication departments at universities mainly teach strategies and tactics for listening comprehension. Listening comprehension refers to methods listeners use to make what they are hearing easier to remember. This is yet another aspect of listening that is the converse of the rhetorical practice for public speaking. In public speaking one arranges a topic, presents logical arguments, and employs stylistic devices to make a speech more understandable and memorable. If an interviewee is so articulate as to communicate with all the rhetorical sophistication of a good public speaker, then there is little need for the interviewer to apply listening comprehension strategies. However, when the interviewee is disorganized, emotional, or uninventive the interviewer needs to repair and dress up the communication to make it memorable and usable. Essentially this means the listener arranges the information as it is being communicated. The listener may also sort out the emotional from the factual, discover the logical arguments, and even attach rhetorical stylistic devices to the information to make it more memorable. Attempting to do all this will almost certainly guarantee that an interviewer will be paying close attention to the interviewee, and it may also drive several of the probing sequences as the interviewer attempts to fill in the gaps and sort out the contradictions.

Some listening comprehension issues can be resolved by managing situation variables. One reason listening requires more effort than reading is that it is easier to be distracted while listening. Reading, by comparison, commands our attention. We pick up a book; we look at the words. We switch reading on or off by our actions. One cannot read two or three things at once. And unless the page is too busy with pictures and artwork, one is not likely to be visually distracted. This is not the case with listening. A coworker calls your house on Saturday to tell you about his frustration working on a project. The high school band is practicing across the street; it sounds like a mangled version of the Star Wars Theme. Now it is drowned out by a loud commercial from the radio. Another phone rings in the distance, and you wonder if someone will answer it. There is a pause. Should you respond now? "That sounds really frustrating. Let me know if I can help." The best way to account for listening distractions is to manage the physical environment. Close the window, turn off WXRT, turn on the answering machine, and go to work constructing meaning from the words of the person who is speaking to you.

Focused Listening

Learning to listen well begins with the realization that we are listening all the time. When we say we are listening to someone, what we really mean is not that we hear him or her, but that we are paying attention to what he or she says. Paying attention does not mean shutting out all other sounds; we can't completely do that. And it does not mean becoming mentally inactive and passively absorbing the other person's words; we can't do that either. Our ears are taking in everything that reaches them, and our minds are always engaged with something. The skill required for focused listening is the ability to make ourselves think about what the other person is saying.

How do we cause ourselves to consider the other person's words? The same way we consider and weigh our own thoughts: we ask ourselves questions. Why is he telling me this? What does she mean? What is being left out? What impact will this have? Almost any question will do. Of course, the best questions are those that will lead to practical or aesthetic observations, but any internal question will cause the mind to engage just as it engages when a book is placed in front of the eyes.

Listening Options and Obstacles

There are only four things that can happen when someone speaks to us. One, we can comprehend nothing. Two, we can focus only on what we want to hear. Three, we can understand what the other person says. And four, we can understand what the other person means. Not comprehending and comprehending only what we want are mainly the result of not paying attention. Understanding what someone says and understanding what someone means are the result of directing our attention.

Just as an iPod can block and override someone's voice, allowing ourselves to concentrate on non-related thoughts can cause us to block messages spoken by others. Dealing with the problem of not hearing someone is simply a matter of focused listening—of paying attention.

Misunderstanding what is said is a much more complex problem because there can never be an absolute understanding of any human statement. Everything we say is subject to interpretation by those around us, and, more importantly, by ourselves. Speaking is a complex psychological and physiological process, and while in a practical sense we can say, "I know what I mean when I say . . ." in fact we would be more accurate if we said, "I think what I mean is . . ." The term Freudian slip refers to a version of this anomaly. A Freudian slip is a message from the subconscious of which the conscious mind is unaware. In truth, every word uttered is a Freudian slip; everything we say is subject to interpretation, and sometimes the audience may understand our words better than we do ourselves.

Audiences, however, have a parallel problem of their own: an unconscious, subversive listening process called hearing what we want to hear. Instead of listening to the other person's message, we tend to look for pieces of the message that we can morph into a message that supports our own beliefs, or perhaps just a message that is more familiar and requires less thought. The best method of countering this tendency is consciously to do the opposite—that is, to identify with the message, to pretend that you are speaking, and that it is your argument. Don't worry; you won't forget who you are and what you believe. As soon as the speaker is finished, your own prejudices and agendas will come flooding back, only now you will communicate more effectively because you have a more intimate understanding of the other.

A similar problem is hearing most of what is said and guessing at the rest. In various ways this happens with all our senses. We see or hear or smell or taste a small part of something and draw conclusions about the whole. It is a necessary cognitive mechanism that helps us make sense of the flood of information we encounter every moment, but it also can lead to problems like stereotyping, misquoting, and misunderstanding. Photographers working with black and white prints have found a very practical application of this phenomenon. If scratches on photographs are touched up with gray dye they will disappear because the mind transposes the colors around them. The substitution tendency occurs in listening on two levels. On one level we fill in for words we did not hear, and on another level we fill in for words we heard and forgot. In both cases it is troublesome.

Filling in the blanks might seem like a good idea, but most of the time it is better not to know something than to think you know something and be wrong. This is particularly problematic when we are listening to someone who is sharing feelings or conveying important information. Teachers, for instance, may not listen to forlorn students because they feel like they have already heard every excuse in the book. But we must remind ourselves: every student is different, and, unless someone has published *The Rhetoric of Excuse Making,* there is no book. Then we can ask ourselves: what is different about this student and this version of the excuse?

The same thing happens when we rely too much on memory. What we see is relatively concrete and stable; what we hear is fleeting. A reader can stare at a sentence until it makes sense, but a listener must remember and study the memory as it fades and becomes reconstituted by the process of remembering. Some people have better audio recall than others, but this is a challenge for all of us. For instance, in the movie *Field of Dreams,* did you hear James Earl Jones say "If you build it, they will come?" You might think you did, but the line is actually "If you build it, he will come." Taking notes and knowing when to take more detailed notes are the main ways to avoid this problem.

Perhaps the best overall strategy for paying attention when listening is humility. We can skirt most of these listening pitfalls if we remind ourselves of our own fallibility, if we let go of the need to defend conclusions and opinions, and if instead we look at the world like children—dwelling on its infinite variations and marvelous unpredictability.

Listening for Content

The main strategy for listening for content is to look for the patterns and relationships that tie what you are hearing together. We hear details, but we remember relationships. It is easier to focus on and remember information if it is part of a story, if it is considered chronologically, or even spatially, or if the words form a pattern like items in a series or rhymes. The best speakers and writers understand this and package their messages accordingly. Little effort is required to remember "Never have so many owed so much to so few," or "I came; I saw; I conquered." It is the artless messages we labor to retain.

It can be argued that all of the canons of rhetoric, all the schemes of repetition, dramatic tactics of delivery, and the clicks and clacks of alliteration are cognitive devices for imprinting messages. This does not mean, however, that communication without rhetorical embellishment is incomprehensible. But if we understand the usefulness of these ancient communication tools and if a book or a speech is devoid of meaningful rhetorical context, then as listeners we can supply them.

As an example, read this list: plate, spoon, violin, cat, dog, cow. Don't reread it. Now count slowly to ten, put the book down, and see how much you remember.

Try it again, only this time read the list in this rich rhetorical context: "Hey diddle, diddle, the cat and the fiddle, the cow jumped over the moon; the little dog laughed to see such a sight, and the dish ran away with the spoon." Count to ten, put the book down, and see how much you can recall now. Did you recall most of it? If you remembered the list better than the nursery rhyme, then you should consider medical school. Most of us do better with the help of alliteration, assonance, rhyme, and the odd narrative context. In fact, some readers may remember the rhyme from when their mothers read it to them. If you remembered it from childhood, think about how long you have retained this nonsense. Probably a lot more than ten seconds have passed since you last heard it, yet you may have remembered it perfectly.

Usually we do not have the energy to turn boring lectures into nursery rhymes. The most practical rhetorical strategy for listening is arrangement. Arrangement is the most important canon to seek in someone else's message. There is simple arrangement and there is meaningful arrangement. Simple arrangement is the standard parts of a discourse, basically introduction, body, conclusion. It may be annoying if an author or speaker ignores these basic listener cues, but they are only conveniences. Meaningful arrangement is the logical or narrative path that one must follow to make the best use of the information. This kind of arrangement provides the context that transforms facts into ideas and messages. The study of rhetoric provides some models, called the modes of discourse: description, narrative or chronology, process analysis, cause and effect, comparison and contrast, definition, and argument. Astute listeners often abstract one or more of these constructs from the jumbled discourse of a less accomplished communicator.

Listening for Emotional Meaning

All human utterance is encoded with both a logical and an emotional meaning. This is what is meant by the adage "what people say and what they mean are often two different things." However, this duality is not limited to communication; it is inherent in every human thought and experience. Awareness of the sometimes fitting, sometimes paradoxical relationship between logic and emotion helps us understand ourselves and the people with whom we interact. Logic and emotion motivate us to participate in interviews—to ask questions and to answer them. A professional interviewer uses this knowledge both to compose the most effective questions and to interpret the answers. Everyone's first inclination is usually to focus on the logical content of interviews, but it is helpful for interviewers to develop listening skills for hearing and interpreting the emotional side of the interview interaction as well. This is listening for emotional meaning.

The natural accumulation of wisdom through experience and a general understanding of psychology are helpful when one needs to contend with the emotional side of the human paradox. When it comes to communication, particularly interviewing, there is one observation about contemporary human behavior that is essential to understand: Ferdinand Tonnies' theory of alienation. Tonnies points out that for most of human history people lived in small communities. They encountered fewer people in their lifetimes than most of us encounter in a week. The pace of their lives was slower, and they came to know their families and neighbors more intimately than those of us who change schools, get married and divorced, move from neighborhood to neighborhood, and shift from job to job if not career to career. Think of Opie Taylor and the other citizens of Mayberry in the old *Andy Griffith Show*. Tonnies believes that each of us has a need to understand and to be understood that is rarely satisfied in contemporary society. Today this unsatisfied need creates almost universal feelings of alienation. Think of James Dean, Bob Dylan, and Kurt Cobain.

Tonnies' theory of alienation explains two key interviewee characteristics: the tendency to avoid answering questions and the potential motivation for voluntary cooperation. We avoid opening up with others because the people around us so quickly go from being strangers to friends to strangers again, because people we trusted used information to take advantage of us, and because there are just so few opportunities to open up. Consequently we have legitimate communication fears and little practice finding and articulating our intimate thoughts. On the other hand, Tonnies teaches us that all interviewees have a pressing desire to be heard. If an interviewer can earn an interviewee's trust it may be possible to release some of the pressure to express oneself.

The key to getting past an interviewee's defenses and opening up the flow of information is simply to let it be known that you are listening. Often we are thinking of what we want to say and not paying complete attention to the other person. We wait for a short pause and then jump in with our own comments. While this may advance your own agenda, it has cut off the other person. Behavior like this is all too common, and it turns conversation into a contest. A minimum of information is exchanged, and there is no opportunity to read emotions beyond the frustration and anxiety caused by the nature of the exchange itself. So, the best way to show you are listening is to put your own agenda aside. Even if the interviewee has a problem and you think you have the solution, bite your tongue and keep listening.

There is only one allowable response when listening for emotional meaning: reflect the emotion you are witnessing at the moment. Note, this may not be the emotion the interviewee is talking about. So if an interviewee says, "I hate the New York Yankees!" but smiles broadly, the empathic response isn't "you *really* don't like them," it is more like "you *enjoy* disliking them!"

When the interviewee's emotional radar senses that the feeling registered and was returned, the reaction is usually a sense of relief accompanied by a desire to go further. A series of empathic responses on a subject of deep emotional meaning can bring out insights about character and behavior that would otherwise be undetectable, even, perhaps, to the interviewee. For instance, if an interviewee says, "My supervisor and I got along ok, I guess," the response that reflects emotional meaning is "you feel conflicted about the relationship." This might invite a comment like,

"He had my best interests in mind, but he didn't (pause), he didn't let me stretch." The interviewer could follow with an emotional meaning response like "this frustrates you." This might invite yet another emotional clue like, "Sometimes it's good to make mistakes, to experiment, to express yourself without having to worry about being corrected or punished." To this, the interviewer might say, "Risk-taking is important to you." An interview like this might cause an employer to realize a job applicant with a spotty employment record could be well worth the risk of a job offer.

It is difficult to focus on emotions and not content. We have so much more practice with content that sometimes we do not even have the words to name the emotions we are feeling or sensing. Becoming attuned to feelings requires practice. This isn't so much interviewing practice as it is practice at being human. After all, life isn't about budget strategies and baseball trades and state-of-the-art computer software. We may fill our days thinking about these things, but the texture of human experience is the play between kindness and insensitivity, selfishness and generosity, hope and despair. Those who recognize this subtext probably perform better at work and certainly lead richer, more fulfilling lives.

Unfortunately, identifying emotions isn't the hardest part of empathic listening. With a little practice, most of us will get acquainted with the lexicon of sentience. The greater challenge has to do purely with communication. It is the difficulty of reflecting the other without betraying our own sentiments and judgments. Remember, the empathic listening process is driven by the release of feelings that have been held back by fear of rejection. Any hint of evaluation in the interviewer's response takes the interviewee out of the emotional sharing mode and into the guarded, practiced façade of argumentation. It is necessary that the response in no way disturb the delicate emotional balance of the moment. It must be in key and on time. And, while the empathic response functions like a question, it may not be a question. Questions by nature shift focus to the intellectual and often create a defensive climate. A true empathic reflection may just be an observation that invites a deeper response without asking for it.

General Listening Skills

Having too much time to think about what is being said can be a problem. One of the reasons the mind tends to wander while listening is that we think faster than we speak. There are time gaps between the words we hear. This space can be used to advantage, or it can be a temptation to wander. By asking yourself questions about what you are hearing, you use the time to affix your attention on the speaker. An old trick is to try to guess what the speaker will say next. This might sound difficult or even distracting, but it will only be difficult at first. Good listening skills will quickly become a habit and require less and less effort.

On the other hand, not having enough time to think about what is being said can be a problem as well. There is little time for contemplation when a subject is too complicated. This can be countered by creating space. When you realize a subject is too difficult to follow, shift your focus away from trying to understand details to understanding more general issues like subject and thesis. The shift to a more easily understood view of the subject should refocus your attention. Of course this means conceding that you will not get the details, but at least it insures that something is gained from the listening experience, and it may keep you from yawning or falling asleep.

Another listening tactic is suspension of disbelief. Sometimes we pass judgment on someone else's statement even before we have heard it. This can be overcome by identifying with the speaker like you might identify with the protagonist in a novel or a movie. Remember, listening is a three-stage process that starts with hearing, becomes understanding, and ends with judgment. It doesn't work very well if these three elements are out of order.

One final point about listening: As consumers we pay for music, movies, books, and professional advice. Doesn't it at least make good fiscal sense to grab, actively and even greedily, all the free information we can get? Think about the comments and arguments that most affected your life. How many of them came in informal conversations with friends, teachers, or even parents? How fortunate you were paying attention! Now, think about all the life-altering information you missed because you let yourself become distracted.

Note-taking

Note-taking can be an effortless byproduct of the interview if the interviewer remembers two things. First, the interviewer is in charge of the interaction. If it takes time to write down a quote and the interviewee has to wait through a few seconds of dead air, so be it. Second, you are taking notes, not making a transcript. These two points work together. If the interviewer is sorting through the information as it is being spoken, then there is no need to write everything on paper. In a one hour interview, maybe only ten or twenty minutes of material are worth keeping. This means that the important information can be written while the interviewee is talking about something else, and most of the time the interviewer isn't writing anything at all. Experienced interviewers and interviewees understand the rhythm of this process. When the interviewee sees that the interviewer is writing, he or she understands the material is important and may volunteer more, and, when the interviewer is not writing, it is a subtle signal that the information may be irrelevant.

Having a feel for the call and response of note-taking can be especially useful if the interviewee says something controversial. Sometimes interviewees get caught up in conversation and say things that they later wish they had not said. However, a journalist or an employment interviewer may find these unguarded comments valuable and want to hear more. In this case, scribbling furiously on a note pad while the interviewee waits is counterproductive. The fact that you are writing may make the interviewee more apprehensive, and if you write at length it creates a pause and gives the interviewee time to reconsider the disclosure. It is preferable in this situation to take casual notes or stop taking notes all together. Then ask the interviewee a non-controversial question and fill in the notes on the previous answer.

Listening for Quotes

When taking notes, it is important to distinguish between a paraphrase of what was said and an actual quote of what was said. Everyone who conducts interviews should be concerned with this, but it is especially important for reporters. It is an absolute standard of professional journalism that if quote marks are used, what follows is a word-for-word transcript of what was actually said. Most note-taking is paraphrase. Quotes are not required in job interviews or sales interviews, and they are used sparsely even in journalistic interviews. The rule of thumb in the journalistic interview is to use the quote if it is either rhetorically interesting or if it is so controversial that it needs the assurance of quote marks to be believable. If a reporter hears a statement worth quoting and writes it down word-for-word, then the reporter should put quote marks around it. If only one word was missed or perhaps was guessed at or assumed, then the reporter should not use quote marks. Later, when the story is being written, when the reporter sees the quote marks, he or she doesn't have to recall the interview and wonder if it is correct. If there are quote marks in the notes, it was captured word-for-word; it can be used in the story.

Sometimes an interviewer may want to write a long quote but gets only half of it. If this happens, do not say to the interviewee, "Could you please repeat that quote about . . .?" This brings too much attention to the subject. Typically when the word "quote" is used, the interviewee will begin to compose a response, and rarely is a self-conscious, composed quote useful. Worse, in a journalistic interview or a job interview, this may imply the interviewee said something wrong and precipitate a carefully constructed and misleading response. If you missed the entire quote, the best thing to do is ask the question again and hope the interviewee gives you the same answer. This works most of the time, but if it doesn't, the interviewer must settle for a paraphrase.

Recording Devices

Recording devices have no place in most interviews. Interviews are conducted to find out what people know or how they behave. This requires a relaxed, contemplative atmosphere. Ideally, most interviews would take place in the interviewee's office or kitchen or workshop with no distractions. This isn't possible most of the time, but it is advantageous for the interviewer to create an atmosphere that is as unobtrusive and calming as possible. Typically in well conducted interviews, the interviewee forgets he or she is talking to an interviewer. The interview transcends into a naturally open, unguarded conversation.

Tape recorders and one-way mirrors radically alter the rhetorical situation. They are constant reminders to the interviewee that this is not a normal conversation, the interviewer is not a friend, and the information being discussed is definitely not going to stay in the room. Typically under these circumstances, interviewees compose their answers. The reaction is similar to what happens when we write or type a note to someone. We become more self-conscious than if we are talking. What we write may be read in circumstances which are different from what we anticipate, and the intended recipient may not be the only one who sees the message. Also, our awareness of conventions further constrains the communication by creating expectations for formality. One advantage of the interview is that it can be conversational: interviewees can express themselves without the concerns that come with writing or public speaking. The insertion of a recording device into this situation only transforms it back into a formal, potentially public forum. Psychologically the effect is similar to what would happen if you asked the interviewee to write down his or her answers and mail them to you.

Deniability and proof are also factors to consider. An interviewee speaking to an interviewer one-on-one can later deny making a statement or can interpret a statement in ways that mitigate an undesirable interpretation. But, if a recording device is present, the interviewee may feel a statement is undeniable. Conversely, this same perception serves as a motivation for interviewers. If they record interviews, then interviewers feel they can never be accused of getting the information wrong. However, in actual practice recordings of statements are still deniable. Sports figures deny making statements all the time, sometimes in spite of the existence of multiple press conference tapes. That is because they know from experience that many fans will hear the denial and not the recording. In court, recorded evidence is refuted routinely on the basis of how it was recorded or the potential for it having been altered or faked. And even if none of these mechanical excuses can be made, the interviewee can always say, "that is not what I meant," or "I misspoke, what I really wanted to say was . . ." In the final analysis, the only predictable impact of using a recording device is that it will give the interviewee cause to hold back information and give the interviewer a false sense of security.

A subtler problem with recording devices is that while they seem to save time during the interview, they add time to the interviewing process as a whole. A one-hour interview takes at least two hours to listen to and transcribe. Then the transcript has to be read and edited down to only the essential information. It could be a four-hour process. An interviewer taking notes is editing and writing the transcript at the same time. The interviewee makes a statement; the interviewer considers it and writes down only what might be useful in the story. Typically only a small percentage of what is discussed needs to be written down. A reporter can finish a one-hour interview, read through the notes, number the paragraphs, write a lead, and type the story in 30 minutes.

Another element of note-taking is that it keeps the interviewer focused. When we write things down we enhance our ability to remember them. That is why taking notes and then typing them up later is one of the best ways to study for an exam. The act of writing engages the mind in a way that is more lasting than just hearing something. An interviewer who is taking notes understands the interviewee better and asks better questions than an interviewer whose main analytical challenge is deciding how close to hold the microphone.

Additionally, the more technology is infused into what is normally an intuitive process, the greater the possibility of error. There is the potential for mechanical failure. With the tape recorder comes a certain dependency. If an interviewer believes the interview is being recorded, there is seemingly no need to take notes and a diminished need to pay close attention to what is said. If the recording device failed to operate, the interviewer has little or nothing to show for the experience.

Moreover, mechanical crutches may really only complicate situations. Rick Markley, a magazine publisher in Chicago, tells a story about when he was freelancing for a magazine called *Indy Car Racing*, and he used a tape recorder in an interview with Michael Andretti. Rick was mainly on vacation when he went to the Indianapolis 500 one year. Just in case an opportunity for a story arose, he brought his press credentials and a brand new tape recorder. The morning before he left for the race, he opened the tape recorder and installed the batteries and a tape. His children and two friends were having peanut butter and jelly at the table. Rick pushed the record button and asked the boys to sing into the built-in microphone. The only song they knew was "Jingle Bells," and they sang it over and over for him. When they were done, Rick played it back. They were way off key; the new tape recorder worked perfectly. He rewound the tape and left for the Brickyard. The drivers were engaged in time trials, and Rick got the opportunity of his young career when he spotted his favorite driver, Michael Andretti, being interviewed by a television reporter and his cameraman. Rick hopped a fence, stepped in front of the television crew, thrust his tape recorder in Andretti's face, hit the button, and stood back recording a story that he couldn't actually hear because of the noise at the track. Rick said it seemed as if Andretti and the other reporter were making faces at him, but he stood his ground. Then the noise died down on the track, and Rick heard "Jingle Bells, Jingle Bells, Jingle all the way . . ." blasting from his tape recorder. He had pushed the wrong button.

Chapter Five

Probing—The Journalistic Interview

Journalistic Interviews

There are two categories of probing interviews: journalistic and behavior-based. Both involve gathering information and observing behavior, but the journalistic interview has collecting information as its goal, while the behavior-based interview has observing behavior as its goal. In other words, the former interview asks what do you know, and the latter asks who are you. Behavior interviews will be discussed in a later chapter; this chapter deals with journalistic interviews.

Almost all qualitative, non-behavioral research interviews are basically journalistic interviews. Researchers perform journalistic interviews in every profession. A series of post-election research interviews might be done by a university professor in the social sciences to study what issues most influenced voters, or a political campaign might perform identical interviews before the election to discover what issues are most salient to voters. The university professor would publish a paper that would be read by students and other faculty to help advance our understanding of democracy, but a campaign staff would use the information to help select issues and plan speeches and advertising to elect a candidate. Both are journalistic research interviews because their focus is on what people know.

Journalistic interviews performed by actual reporters differ usually in that they are more narrowly focused; sometimes they look for just a single fact. However, a small percentage of journalistic interviews have almost as broad a focus as academic research. The term for these larger interview projects is "investigative journalism." Investigative journalists might conduct a series of interviews using methods identical to those used by researchers in the social sciences. Here one rarely conducts a single research interview. Investigative journalists and social scientists conduct series of interviews to gain a broader and deeper perspective of an issue. For example, a beat reporter might interview a police detective to find out what kind of weapon was used in a shooting. A social scientist or an investigative reporter might interview several detectives about shootings over a six month period to study the effects of easily obtainable handguns.

Some of the fields actively involved in journalistic research interviewing might surprise you. One is computer programming. Rarely does someone design software for his or her own needs. Software engineering is a profession that creates tools for other professions. A software developer might be working with doctors and hospital administrators on one project, and then with human resource managers on the next project. Even if both projects involve healthcare, the needs of the end users would be significantly different. This means that the software engineer not only has to be skilled in programming languages, but also has to be skilled in research, particularly in conducting the journalistic interview.

One might wonder, how complicated can this be? You ask people what their needs are; they tell you, and you give them what they want. Unfortunately, people do not always know what they want. Furthermore, even if a client knows what he or she wants, you still have to work to get the information. Even successful people may have trouble prioritizing, keeping schedules, staying on the topic, and articulating their own thoughts. Information gathering benefits from preparation by versatile, well-trained interviewers who can come back with valuable information regardless of what peculiar obstacle was presented by a given interviewee.

The Journalistic Guide

As with any probing interview, a guide of topics should be assembled and arranged prior to the interview. However, the more one conducts interviews on a subject, the more one knows about it and the better one is at writing an interview guide. To take full advantage of this, an interviewer needs a flexible guide. In most cases conducting one or two exploratory interviews to gather topic information for the guide is useful. In research that requires a series of interviews, the guide might evolve from interview to interview. As a series of interviews progresses, the interviewer can retain the most useful topics and substitute other topics that were suggested by the research itself.

To develop a journalistic research guide, consider the topic, the interviewee, and what you most want to find out. Make a list of subjects to explore, and arrange them in the order that seems best suited to the anticipated logical and emotional development of the interview. Then practice the interview using the guide. Find a test interviewee and ask him or her to answer the questions honestly. The honesty requirement is essential. If a test interviewee is making up answers, then there has been no test. There is little need to practice reading from a guide. One practices *probing* from an interviewer guide. If the answers are make-believe, then no probing has taken place.

Lastly, much of the research in the social sciences is quantitative. It should be noted that the methods suggested here—working from a guide instead of a schedule, letting the guide evolve over time, and spontaneous probing—are incompatible with most quantitative research. Quantitative research attempts to draw conclusions based on comparable data from multiple sources. When questions change from interviewee to interviewee, a comparison of answers will provide no inferences for a target population. The methods required for quantitative research will be discussed in the survey chapter.

The Schedule of Questions

A probing interview works best from a guide of topics, but sometimes it is necessary to have some of the questions written in advance. Reporters, for instance, memorize a schedule of generic questions that must be answered for all news stories. Perhaps you are already familiar with it: who, what, where, when, why, and how. This schedule has its roots in classical rhetoric, where it was used to explore topics centuries before the advent of objective journalism. It is also the basis of Kenneth Burke's pentad where it forms a list of questions to be used to analyze public discourse and rhetorical situations. Burke's pentad is made up of act (what), scene (where and when), agent (who), agency (how), and purpose (why). While these questions might not always be useful, they do provide a mental checklist for the exploration of almost any issue, and they insure that a reporter will not return to the newspaper office with only a partial story.

The almost inevitable problem is that an interviewer working from a list of questions instead of a guide of topics will rely too much on routine and not probe past the anticipated information. Flexibility of pursuit is what makes the probing interview a powerful research tool. The guide is helpful without being constraining. Knowing there is a check-list allows the interviewer the freedom to concentrate fully on interviewee responses. Follow-up questions and even supplemental guide items will be suggested by the discourse itself. A veteran reporter or a seasoned interviewer will automatically consider questioning options like who, what, where, when, why, and how as the opportunities arise and may review them along with the guide before closing the interview. Thus, a skilled journalist or researcher needs only the guide of topics as a reminder of what to cover.

If a schedule of questions is necessary, do not write it until after writing the guide of topics. Writing a guide is an analytical process, and writing a schedule is a creative process. The analysis must come first. Ask yourself: what do I need to know? Then put on the creative thinking cap and ask yourself: how can I find this out? Anyone who skips the guide step will likely end up with a list of interesting questions that is redundant and leaves out important information. Overall, schedules of questions are problematic in qualitative research. It is better to work from a guide and trust your ability to follow clues left by the interviewee.

Ethical Requirements

Research interviewers, particularly reporters, need to tell interviewees who they are, what they are looking for, and how they plan to use the information. It might be as simple as "My name is Tom Roach, I am a reporter for the *Star-Tribune*, and I would like to talk to you about . . ." Yes, there are times when this rule needs to be suspended, like in a criminal investigation. However, when exceptions are being considered, they should be discussed first with an editor or a research committee.

Another ethical consideration is off-the-record comments. If a reporter or researcher agrees a comment is off the record, it must remain that way. The only way out of an off-the-record agreement is not to make it in the first place. Interviewers use their understanding of social rules to create exigence to motivate interviewees to share information. This often causes conflict for the interviewee. On the one hand, the interviewee may know and trust a reporter and want to cooperate, but on the other hand, the information may be offensive or damaging or embarrassing. Many times an interviewee wants to solve the problem by giving the information but asking that the reporter or researcher not use it. This is a wonderful psychological solution for the interviewee, but it is an absurd option for a reporter. There is little point in conducting the interview if the information cannot be used. Once an agreement like this is made, all interviewing strategies and skills are useless. In most cases it is better to tell the interviewee you want only information you can use, and then go after it.

Occasionally interviewees will find themselves volunteering information without constraint and then regret it. This might lead to a comment like, "by the way, that's off the record." Interviewers may agree to this after-the-fact reclassification, but ethically they are not required to acknowledge a request to which they never agreed. If preserving or building rapport with the source is more important, then it might seem desirable to agree, but it sets a bad precedent. What happens if later the source reveals something that you intend to use? The interviewee will say, "That's off the record," and you have to say, "I didn't agree to that." This is problematic because you participated in a pattern of interviewer-interviewee interaction that allowed the interviewee to review comments and then retract them. Now you are changing the rules. The best policy if an interviewee makes an after-the-fact censorship attempt is to say, "No; I didn't agree to that."

Are off-the-record deals ever desirable? It may be worth considering an off-the-record offer if the information promises to lead to other sources who will make similar statements on the record. This is a slippery slope, however. Often the interviewer goes from interviewee to interviewee without getting anyone to talk on the record. This was the case with much of the Watergate reporting done by Bob Woodward and Carl Bernstein. It drove them to use unnamed sources who their critics said didn't exist. Woodward and Bernstein's data turned out to be true, but their methods made it possible for a corrupt government to make plausible arguments that cast doubts on their work.

Another problem with offering to take comments off the record is that a court of law may not honor your agreement. Judges sometimes force reporters to choose between loyalty to their profession and loyalty and obedience to the law. Most judges and law enforcement officials believe that no one is above the law, and they will not hesitate to put a reporter in jail for refusing to cooperate. An investigative interviewer in most other professions is ethically justified in revealing sources or information if required to by a court. This is not the case with a reporter. When reporters exercise their rights to free speech by gathering and publishing information, and when those rights would be impeded by the legal system, then reporting is, literally, above the law. A judge might demand information out of concern for the rights of a citizen in a particular trial, but a reporter withholds information to protect the rights of all citizens. Attorneys may feel that free speech is equal to other rights like the right to a fair trial, but history shows that free speech is not a privilege made possible by democratic governments. Democracy is the privilege, and it is made possible by free speech. Reporters who take information off the record should do so knowing that it may cause them to spend time in jail, not just because they are professionals, but because they are patriots.

Probing

Learning to ask questions is easy, but one can spend a lifetime developing skills to ask questions strategically—to probe. In this way, interviewing is similar to chess. Chess has very few rules and can be learned quickly. A professor might teach his five-year-old son Carl to move the pieces but then beat him easily. The professor can play a friend, Peter, who is a member of a chess club, and Peter easily beats the professor. Peter is easily beaten by a visiting chess master, Jennifer. Jennifer is beaten by a tournament champion, Susan. Susan is beaten by the Russian chess champion, Boris, and Boris is beaten by a computer, Hal. Interestingly, Boris the Russian chess champion doesn't know much more about the rules of chess than the five-year-old Carl. His vastly superior playing ability is due to an understanding of strategic options and possible outcomes. Similarly, almost everyone knows how to conduct an interview, but there are levels upon levels of rhetorical options and psychological insights. The study of interviewing is not about learning to ask questions; it is about learning to ask them strategically.

Probing is guided by a few principles. *First, stay on track.* What is the track? The track is not the interview topic. The track is a liberally defined body of knowledge that includes the topic. On the one hand staying on track means always keeping the topic in sight, but on the other hand, it means not limiting the dialogue to only the obvious or most significant issues. Interviewing is not merely conversation and it is not a mechanical exchange of data; it lies in-between. An interviewer engages in conversation and offers friendship for the purpose of gaining information. If the relationship between interviewer and interviewee begins to take the interview too far away from the topic, the interviewer needs to be disciplined and refocus the dialogue, even if it means stepping back from an emotionally rewarding interaction. Conversely, when the interviewer takes the interviewee into stressful territory, and the interviewee appears to be losing the desire to cooperate, the interviewer may need to end an otherwise productive line of questioning and briefly shift to a friendlier, though potentially less meaningful, exchange.

A second principle is keep the interview focused on the interviewee. The interviewee should do most of the talking. A good interviewer will talk only about 10 percent of the time. A 30-70 exchange might be acceptable in difficult circumstances, but if the interview is a 50-50 exchange it fails. It fails not because it wastes time, although it does. The interview fails because the interviewer has unnecessarily influenced the outcome. No interviewer can be absolutely objective, but one who talks as much as the interviewee will impact the dialogue in ways that could have been avoided by a professionally sparse approach. Keep the focus on the interviewee. Use the interview to discover the interviewee's agenda, not as a vehicle to advance your own. If an interviewer inserts his or her opinions into the interview it should be because they were needed to build trust, spark a reaction, or for some other strategic reason. If an interviewer talks more than the interviewee, or influences the interviewee, then in the final analysis, it was the interviewer who was interviewed, and the data produced is worse than useless; it is misleading.

A third principle is never be satisfied with an answer. Always ask a follow-up question, and don't move on until the interviewee's lack of meaningful information makes it necessary. Interviewing is a dynamic progression. If the last answer was good, then the potential for the next one is even better. A common mistake among interviewers is to feel satisfied when they get what they were looking for, or when an unexpected response is particularly meaningful. The metaphor for the wrong approach might be shopping. You find what you are looking for and go home. A better metaphor is mining. If a mining company finds a small vein of gold, it follows it hoping it leads to bigger and bigger veins, and that is exactly what an interviewer should do.

Every question that can be open should be open. This fourth principle is the most difficult to follow because closed questions are so easy and tempting to ask. A full discussion of open questions can be found in Chapter Three. Mainly, we ask open questions to keep the dialogue alive; closed questions truncate it. When a closed question is asked and answered, there is a sense of finality that makes continuing a line of probing difficult. Open questions have the opposite effect—they forecast a prolonged dialogue. When an interviewee answers an open question, there is a sense that the answer is one of many building blocks and that it will only partially resolve the exigence. The interviewee answers the question with an eye to developing the idea further. Sometimes interviewees will correct the interviewer and say, "a better question might be . . ." This is a good sign; it means an open question atmosphere has been sustained, and the interviewee is as caught up in the exchange as the interviewer.

Unfortunately knowing you should ask open questions doesn't make it easier to ask them. Most of us think in terms of closed questions. This makes sense when we ask questions of ourselves. Because we are interviewer and interviewee, we tend to know where we are going. Also, closed questions are focused; they help us concentrate. And closed questions are emotionally more satisfying than open questions. This is because open questions create more of an exigence, making them emotionally taxing. While open questions force an interviewee to work harder, closed questions create comfort because they imply agreement. Closed questions may not use subjective language like "don't you agree" or "if you are like me, you believe . . ." but they imply it. All of this provides habit and emotional incentive to avoid open questions. Consequently open questions require vigilance, discipline, and practice.

Always move toward the stasis point is the fifth principle. Stasis, as discussed earlier, refers to the point at which the argument rests. If a political candidate tells a reporter, "I try to follow most of the campaign spending restrictions," the best follow up isn't "Why do you think campaign spending restrictions are important?" The interviewee has just admitted to a crime; the question that pursues the stasis point is: "Can you give me an example of a campaign spending restriction that you don't always follow?" Identifying and tracking the stasis point is difficult sometimes even for experienced professionals. In the 1980s, David Stockman, President Ronald Reagan's budget director, told the *Atlantic Monthly* that the administration's budget was driven by campaign rhetoric and that "we never added up the numbers." The stasis points were the competence of the presidential staff and the effects of an unrealistic budget on the economy. The Washington press core followed up on the Stockman story with a frenzy of interviews with members of the administration and Congress and somehow managed to miss the stasis point by developing a news narrative about how the admission would affect Stockman's career.

Public Relations Interviews

Public relations professionals conduct journalistic interviews and write news stories in the form of press releases. The journalistic interview for them should be conducted exactly as it would be conducted by a reporter. The only difference is that the public relations interviewer works for the interviewee or the interviewee's company, and when the interview is over it may be required that the interviewer rewrite or author parts of the interview data.

While the process of interviewing and writing the story might be the same for journalists and public relations professionals, journalism and public relations have almost antithetical roles in the public sphere. Most newspapers since the 1950s have marketed themselves as objective sources of information. That claim is based on a process of news-gathering and writing that requires the reporter to omit his or her opinion to the extent that it is humanly possible. A reporter changing or inventing quotes damages the reputation of the newspaper and the profession. At most newspapers this is a good way to get fired.

Public relations professionals use the same skills as journalists. In fact about one third of all public relations practitioners are former journalists. But their jobs are significantly different because they work for people or companies with a public profile—news sources or news subjects. Anyone who becomes a source or subject of news coverage has the right to employ professional communicators to help develop public statements, much as someone in a court case can seek help from an attorney. A public relations professional might write a speech, coach a client before a press conference, or draft a public announcement. All of these things could be reported in a news story written by a reporter, or they could be reported in a press release written by a public relations professional. In the case of the press release, however, the public relations professional is sometimes both generating the story and reporting it.

The reporter and the news source are necessarily different roles in the profession of journalism; for the public relations professional they can be one. Consequently, there are fewer ethical constraints if the public relations professional wants to rewrite an interviewee's answer, or even make up some quotes without conducting an interview. The main ethical considerations here are the veracity of the information and the permission of the source. However, while it may not be unethical, making up an interview is not a good practice. The best information will come from an actual interview with the only person who is the expert. Good press releases start with an interview conducted just the way an objective journalist would conduct it. Revisions can be made later, but in the long run, actually conducting the interview probably takes less time and produces more interesting copy.

Broadcast News Interviews

Broadcast journalists, like public relations professionals, would benefit from following the interview process used by professional journalists. Research the story, prepare a guide, conduct the interview.

The reputation of the news industry has been in decline for the last quarter century due to management policies that have removed the firewall between advertising departments and newsrooms, strategic high-profile attacks from U.S. presidents and presidential candidates, and some notable examples of newspaper reporters inventing interview data and even fictional interviewees. However, a more subtle but perhaps more significant factor contributing to a decline in trust during this period is the unprofessional behavior of television reporters and the public tendency to lump professional print journalists together with uncredentialed, untrained television personalities under the heading of news media.

In the years where all news was carried in newspapers or on the radio, the interview took place behind the scenes. Newspaper reporters traditionally were assigned beats where they developed a professional rapport with their sources. Rarely would a shouting match occur between a print reporter and an interviewee, but if it did, it happened out of sight of newspaper readers. The public saw only an edited, sanitized story and probably assumed it was the result of a cordial, rational interaction. With the advent of television news the interview became the story. Viewers now see television reporters harassing their sources and redundantly asking "How does it feel?" on almost any occasion. Often there is little distinction between the behavior of the people in the crowd screaming and waving at the camera and the behavior of the person holding the microphone. In the long run, everyone employed in the news-gathering profession would benefit if broadcast interviews were just as well prepared and well executed as those conducted by print journalists.

Chapter 6

The Journalistic Interviewee

The Power Equation

Contemporary life is dominated by ideas and words. While traditional power mechanisms like violence or wealth still impact our lives, they are increasingly subordinated by the power of rhetoric. Clearly information is the world's most valuable commodity, and acquiring and disseminating information is a primary means of exercising power in the 21st century. In strict power terminology, the interviewer exercises power in acquiring information, and the interviewee exercises power by disseminating it. However, the person with the information obviously holds the most power, and that is probably why traditional rhetorical studies have looked mainly at only this half of the equation. Aristotle, Cicero, and Quintillion theorized about ways people who have information can package it and transmit it for greatest impact. This study of interviewing is somewhat unique in that it reveals the acquisition of information as a parallel rhetorical act. All of the preceding chapters have articulated ways in which rhetoric may be used by the interviewer, who in classical terms was the audience, to abstract information from the interviewee, who in classical terms was the speech-giver. That is, they have detailed rhetorical methods for the listener to control the rhetorical situation by manipulating the setting, naming the subject, setting the tone, arranging the speech, and even selecting the interviewee-speaker in order to acquire information.

This chapter re-inverts the power arrangement. It explores how the interviewee can take control of the interview. While experience may tell us this is not possible, the prospect of the interviewee controlling the interview is not so preposterous when one considers that the interviewee is the one with the desired information, and therefore the party with the most power. The interviewee is, after all, the speech-giver.

News Source Strategy

Few interviewees have as much potential power over the interview as does the news source. The news source may or may not want to share information with a reporter. The reporter, on the other hand, needs the information. It doesn't matter if a reporter has been sent to Washington, D.C., to cover the president or is assigned the police beat in Kansas City, the job is the same: develop news sources, gather information, write stories. If no information is gathered, no stories are written and the reporter gets reassigned or terminated. The key strategic objective for a news reporter is not to write well, it is to cultivate news sources to get information. The key strategic objective for the news source is to use the power of information-giving to manipulate the interview and even have some influence on the printed or broadcast story.

In order to gain some control over the interview situation, news interviewees need to assess the situation from the reporter's point of view. What is newsworthy here? What information is essential to the story? Is there any information for which I am the only possible source? What happens if I do or do not cooperate? Then the situation needs to be assessed from the interviewee's point of view. What do I have to gain or lose from an interview? What information is harmless to me and my organization, and what information is detrimental? How will public perception of me and my organization change as a result of sharing or not sharing certain information?

Whistle Blowing

It is important to note that while reporters and news sources are usually negotiating the exchange of information as professionals, they sometimes need to exchange information because they are citizens. The moral and ethical imperatives of citizenship outweigh concerns for personal gain or loss. If an employee of a company knows of company activities that are illegal or harmful to the general public, then reporting that information to the appropriate authorities or leaking it through the news media may need to be done without hesitation and in spite of personal risk.

Weighing the Options

The interview process provides information for news stories, which provide information that builds public narratives, or in the broadest sense, reputations. Reporters, then, are not the desired audience. The only reason to grant an interview with a reporter is to get information out to the general public to impact, ultimately, the narrative. In most cases this is an easy task. If a hospital is investing in a new form of cancer treatment and you are an oncologist, then you have some compelling reasons to grant an interview. The story narrative could be that health care professionals are using new technology to save lives. The interview presents almost no risk and represents an opportunity to educate the public and promote your career, so you grant it. But sometimes public opinion and the story narrative make the interview disadvantageous to the interviewee. If another hospital in the community is considered the main cancer treatment center, then the new cancer treatment story narrative might be about competition and marketing strategies and rising hospital costs. Public relations minded news sources seek out opportunities like the first one and avoid opportunities where the risks are greater and the potential returns are diminished.

The news source interviewee also should consider the professionalism and the credibility of the interviewer and the interviewer's news organization. Newspaper reporters are the most credible interviewers. Reporters for the prestige dailies are trained professionals who are held accountable to journalistic ethics by their editors, their peers, and their readers. At the other extreme, local television reporters have minimal constraints over what they do with a story, and they have little to no influence over what their news station does with their footage once it is turned in. The difference for the interviewee is having a *New York Times* reporter accept a jail sentence rather than reveal your name, or having an editor at CBS rerecording and splicing in new versions of the questions you were asked and changing the context of the interview.

Sometimes news sources have little or no choice in these matters. If you are already part of a news story, then you probably have to speak to the news media. When the story will be told with or without your cooperation, the only choices are having other people tell your story for you or telling your side of the story yourself. Companies and public figures who decide not to talk to the news media, usually find their fortunes going from bad to worse. That is because reporters writing about conflict have two objectives: cover the news and look for at least two opposing sources. But the first objective is the most important one. Thus, not talking to the news media will not prevent the news media from covering the story. Once they have offered to conduct an interview and the interview has been refused, they are free to print or broadcast whatever they have. This means that the public, instead of hearing two sides in a controversial story, gets all of its information from your opponents, who if they are smart, will try to make it seem as if there is only one way to look at the issue. About the only time it is advantageous not to talk to the news media is when you are the only possible source and by not talking, you effectively shut down the narrative.

The Interviewee's Guide

Once the interview has been granted, the interviewee should prepare an interview guide. The guide should list all the topics the interviewee wants to discuss. The interviewer also has a guide, which is essentially a list of topics for questions. The interviewee should anticipate this guide and conform to it as much as possible. A successful interviewee guide won't be able to change the subject, but might be able to shift the emphasis. The interviewer's guide is used to control the sequencing and the focus of question-asking. The interviewee's guide is essentially a list of possible answers. It cannot change the arrangement of the interview, but it can change the tone of the interview. When the interviewer needs to be aggressive, the interviewee needs to be patient. The interviewee should review the guide items and practice talking about them. Reporters want stories with details, so each of the guide items should have one or more stories associated with it, and the interviewee should be fluent in telling these stories. Then every time the interviewer asks a question from the interviewer guide, the interviewee considers if there is an answer from the interviewee guide that fits it. If there is, the interviewee tells the story, makes the point, and the reporter records it.

Cooperation

It is usually not advantageous to refuse to answer a question. The key to establishing rapport with a reporter is cooperativeness. Reporters covering conflict stories are used to being treated rudely, and they appreciate when someone is open and candid with them. Being cooperative is not as difficult as it might sound. The key is simply always to answer the question. This doesn't mean you have to tell the reporter everything you know, however. Let's say you are the company Public Relations spokesperson, there has been a fire at your oil refinery, and the corporate attorneys have forbidden you from discussing the possible causes of the fire.

Here's an example of what not to do:

> Spokesperson: "All I can give you right now are the names of some of the injured employees."
>
> Reporter: "What was the cause of the fire?"
>
> Spokesperson: "I can't talk about the cause of the fire."
>
> Reporter: "Did it have something to do with the age of this facility?"
>
> Spokesperson: "I can't answer that."
>
> Reporter: "Are you considering negligence as a possible cause?"
>
> Spokesperson: "Look, I said I can't answer that. Do you have any other questions or is this interview over?"

The problem with this pattern of responses is the spokesperson is actually creating hostility not defusing it, and he or she has not taken advantage of the opportunity to contribute positive information to the story. This approach forces the reporter to look for other sources like a union representative, or an angry neighbor perhaps. Now, here is an example of how not to compromise the protected information, but still answer the questions:

> Reporter: "What was the cause of the fire?"
>
> Spokesperson: "Our safety team is looking into that, but I do not have anything to report yet."
>
> Reporter: "Did it have something to do with the age of this facility?"
>
> Spokesperson: "The facility is 42 years old, but it is inspected every six months by our safety team and every year by the Whiting fire department. I can tell you we have an aggressive policy of repairing and replacing anything that might malfunction, particularly if that malfunction could be a threat to life and property."
>
> Reporter: "Are you considering negligence as a possible cause?"
>
> Spokesperson: "It is only prudent to consider that possibility, but we are pretty safety conscious here. In the last year every employee at the plant, from the plant manager to truck drivers, went through six hours of safety training."

If the reporter asks what equipment was replaced recently, the interviewee should be ready with a description and costs. If the reporter asks, "How do you define 'safety conscious?'", then the interviewee should be able to quote a definition from the mission statement or a memo or a safety training class. If the interview is handled right, chances are that the story narrative will be about how the company was prepared and sustained minimal damage. Handled poorly, the story could be about the threat that the plant presents to the community.

Speaking Off the Record

There is a simple rule to follow when talking to reporters: Never say anything that you do not want to see printed or broadcast. It is true that some members of the journalistic profession will honor an off the record agreement, even if it requires they defy a court order. The problem with entering into an off the record agreement is that it requires predicting someone else's behavior. Consider all the things that can go wrong. The reporter intends to keep the off the record agreement, but tells another reporter or an editor who uses the information and leaks your name. Perhaps you make the agreement with a well-meaning reporter who succumbs to pressure from editors or the courts. Or, the reporter confuses the information with printable information and uses it anyway. Most reporters are honest to a fault, but what if you disclosed information to one who is unscrupulous and threatens to expose you if you do not provide additional information? This list could go on and on. If you make an off the record agreement and disclose volatile information, the potential problems you face are almost uncountable. If you refuse to disclose the information only one thing can go wrong: the reporter will be frustrated and upset. So what? Remember, you have the information. In the long run they need you more than you need them.

The only practical use of talking off the record is to build rapport by sharing nonthreatening information or to slow the spread of information that you would have disclosed anyway. News sources share non-controversial information tips with reporters all the time. A university president might mention that plans are being considered to build a new student center, but say that it cannot be discussed publicly until the board of trustees brings it up at a meeting. There is little incentive for a reporter to alienate this important news source to break a building construction story. And, if the reporter does violate the trust and break the story, no real damage is done.

The sharing of controversial information that you know will come out anyway is a little trickier. Let's say the university has suddenly decided it needs to raise tuition. The university board is acting in an arbitrary manner. No public meetings have been held, and no feedback solicited; the announcement will drop like a bomb on the academic community. Leaking the information slowly may be the only way the chancellor has of lessening the impact. Telling a student reporter off the record that the university is planning to raise tuition significantly, the chancellor knows the information will probably pass into circulation. It may start as a rumor, then be discussed in a speculative editorial, and finally appear in a news story after the student has turned up a source who is willing to go on the record. If the student prints the story immediately, well, the announcement had to be made, you had nothing to lose.

It should be noted there are ethical and unethical ways to leak information. Requiring a reporter to promise to keep the information quiet when you really want it to be spread is unethical. If however, you say something like, "It would be difficult for me if this were to get out right now, but . . ." then there is a mutual understanding that you are cooperating with the reporter and you would appreciate if the reporter would cooperate with you by not rushing the story into print.

Third Face of Power Tactics

Making an argument is the first face of power. It is what we do when we write essays or give speeches. Setting the agenda is the second face of power. Developing a guide for the interview is an exercise of the second face of power. Manipulating the rules of the discourse is the third face of power. This is done by creating or calling attention to rules like noting that the allotted time for the interview has expired or claiming that a particular question is not on the topic. Each face of power trumps the face before it. Normally if two people present arguments, the better argument wins. If, however, the person with the weaker argument sets the agenda, it may be possible to eliminate the better argument from the discourse. But someone controlling the rules of the discourse can prevent arguments from being heard and override agenda setting tactics. Because the interview is governed mainly by social rules, and because those rules are mostly tacit, the interview is highly vulnerable to third face of power tactics.

A good example of all three faces of power can be seen in the notorious live interview between 1988 presidential candidate George Bush and CBS anchorman Dan Rather. Bush defended his role in the Iran Contra scandal, reminded Rather that the interview was supposed to be about his campaign, not Iran Contra, and accused Rather of not acting professionally. The argument defending his actions was first face of power. When Bush had exhausted it, and Rather refused to change the subject, Bush used second face of power by saying they were supposed to talk about the campaign. Rather was persistent, and Bush responded by calling attention to Rather's unprofessional behavior. The claim of unprofessionalism essentially argues that Rather is violating the rules of engagement between a reporter interviewer and a news source interviewee, particularly the rule that calls for objectivity on the reporter's part.

Any interviewee can use third face of power tactics. The attack on reporter objectivity is usually the most potent. If a reporter is unrelenting in pursuit of information you choose not to discuss, an effective third face of power tactic might be to say, "It seems like you have already decided what you want me to say and are trying to force me to say it." Or, a more direct application might be: "Aren't you supposed to be fair and objective? It seems like you have already formed an opinion about this." Journalists tend to respond by overcompensating when their objectivity is challenged. After Bush attacked Rather on live television, the news media spent two weeks broadcasting roundtable discussions evaluating their own ethics. In the process they dropped the ball on the Iran Contra story, and Bush was elected president without having to explain his role in the scandal.

The Reporter Source Relationship

The ideal relationship with a reporter is one where you are viewed as a reliable source of information. The keys to this are never be dishonest or misleading and never hesitate to respond. Reporters, like police, often have to deal with social problems the rest of us don't see. The world from their point of view can seem dichotomous. There are good people who have nothing to hide and always tell the truth, and there are rascals who live by guile—hiding, lying, and taking advantage of anyone who lets them. Reporters will protect their valued sources, and they will work relentlessly to expose the rascals. The best advice for someone in the news is to stay on the good side of the equation.

If there is a middle ground, it is represented by the best of the public relations practitioners. They see themselves as honest advocates for their clients, and most seasoned reporters respect this stance. It means the public relations professional is positioned like an attorney who makes the best ethical argument possible and goes no further. Reporters know that sources like this are only giving them one side of the story, but they also know it is trustworthy. Most of the interviewee tactics above fall into this category. They are for interviewees who are seen as honest advocates. This allows for an adversarial but professional and respectful relationship, but leaves the interviewee in a position where he or she can still vie for control of the news narrative with the reporter.

The Press Conference

There is no better example of the power sharing between speaker and audience than the press or media conference. Let's say a candidate for president appears at his or her party's national convention and gives a speech. This is the classical rhetorical relationship of speaker and audience. The speaker controls the setting, the subject, the arrangement, and the tone of the discourse. Now, let's say the candidate receives the nomination from the convention and is interviewed by a reporter from the *Chicago Tribune*. The speaker–audience relationship is inverted because now the interviewer–audience has control of the setting, the subject, the arrangement, and the tone of the discourse, even though the interviewee-speaker is still sending the message and the audience is still receiving it. Later in the campaign, when the candidate holds a press conference, the roles are reinverted. The candidate is essentially an interviewee, yet he or she reacquires control of setting, subject, arrangement, and tone. In the press conference, the roles of speaker and interviewee are completely integrated as are the roles of audience and interviewer.

Anyone who has taken a speech class understands how a speaker exercises power, and the previous chapters explain how the interviewer can shift the power equation in favor of the audience, but how does the press conference shift power back to the interviewee? It is done by exercising all of the control of one giving a speech.

First, the interviewee selects the physical setting. Some settings tip the power balance in favor of the interviewer and some in favor of the interviewee. Presidents giving press conferences in the White House press room are mostly at the mercy of reporters. They have to call on someone, and once they do, they have to address the question. But when they are walking to the Air Force One helicopter, there is no expectation to call on anyone. This is because the reporters are officially there to see the President board the aircraft and because the helicopter engines make it difficult to hear. If the president wants to talk about social security, but the news media is only interested in the Iraq conflict, then there may never be a social security question at the press conference. At the helicopter, however, the reporters, instead of raising their hands and saying "Mr. President," are actually shouting out their questions in an effort to get his attention. If eight reporters are shouting about Iraq and one enterprising reporter mentions social security, the president can choose not to hear the Iraq questions, but stop and address the one on social security. Handlers of presidents have understood for years that the walk to the helicopter is basically an interviewee controlled press conference.

Another aspect of physical setting is its visual rhetorical value. Most people get their news from television, and the image they see often makes a greater impression than what they hear. A press conference interviewee can take advantage of this when choosing a setting. If the interviewee wants to downplay the story, the press conference can be scheduled in a cavernous room. Whenever the room is larger than the crowd the visual rhetorical message is there was little interest. If, however, the candidate wants to promote an issue at a press conference, then it can be scheduled in a room that does not quite fit the expected crowd. The visual message will be of people fighting for space and working to get close to the speaker.

The press conference interviewee may also be able to control the tone of the discourse by carefully choosing which reporters to call on. If a company has to call a press conference because of a plant accident or a scandal, it will face two kinds of reporters. The larger group will be unknown reporters from out of town or from beats that usually don't bring them into contact with the organization. A smaller group of reporters will be the local reporters or the reporters covering the company's beat. A Chicago reporter covering a plant accident in Joliet has no relationship with the person conducting the press conference and will likely never see him or her again. A local reporter may be acquainted with the public relations person behind the microphones: they may have worked together on stories and may do so again. The out of town reporter has nothing to lose and is most likely to ask impolite and inflammatory questions; the local reporter is more likely to give the company the benefit of the doubt and ask questions in a more cordial manner. The astute press conference interviewee will survey the audience, identify the safest reporter interviewers, and call on them first. After three or four somewhat respectful question–answer interactions, a tone has been established and, when the speaker begins to call on the unknown reporters, it is more likely they will behave as professionally as their local counterparts.

Tone can also be established with the way the press conference interviewee takes questions. Remember, the interviewee is the person with the most rhetorical power because he or she holds the information that the interviewers want. Reporter interviewers will do whatever they deem necessary to get that information. If, as is often the case, the press conference interviewee calls on a reporter who is screaming and waving, then more reporters will be screaming and waving when it is time to take the next question. Someone conducting a press conference in this manner is actually using reward and recognition to train the interviewers to be hostile. A better method is to raise your hand and say, "Who has the first question?" Most of the crowd may start shouting, but someone will quickly catch on and raise a hand. If you call on that person, answer the question, then raise your hand and say, "Next question," other reporters will have figured out this is the best way to get your attention and they will raise their hands too. Chances are, if you call on someone who has quietly raised a hand again, by the time you get to the third or fourth question all the reporters will be raising their hands like school children.

Invention and arrangement are particularly problematic for press conference interviewees. You may control who you call on for a while, and you may be able to establish tone, but what interviewer reporters ask and when they ask it are entirely at their discretion. A method of partially overcoming this problem is to make a planned statement at the beginning of the press conference. In other words, completely revert to the speaker-audience model. This is not uncommon, and reporter interviewers will usually show patience if the speech isn't too long. This gives the press conference interviewee an opportunity to present a thesis and use arrangement to develop it. The tactic requires a degree of forethought and discipline. Typically interviewees who use the strategy of starting with a statement try to shift the subject. This is a foolish mistake. Reporters are professionals; they will not forget what is newsworthy and why they are there. Any attempt to shift focus will only create animosity. A wise interviewee will do what firefighters sometimes do with forest fires: go to the hottest point and try to exhaust it. This accomplishes two things. One, it shows that you are not trying to hide something and relieves the audience's emotional pressure to drag you to the stasis point and expose you. Two, there is a social rule that you don't ask people a question if they just gave you the answer. If the opening statement is done right, the reporter interviewers may themselves move the discourse off the stasis point. Thus, the key issues will have been covered mainly in the speech portion of the press conference where you had control of invention and arrangement.

Another preliminary step that draws on traditional speaker-oriented rhetorical theory is making the ethical appeal. Aristotle and most of the rhetorical theorists who followed him believed that whether or not the audience trusted the speaker was more important than any argument he or she could make. Aristotle thought this could be accomplished by telling the audience how knowledgeable and honest and well-meaning you are, but this is unacceptable in a post-Christian society where humility has become part of the character construct. The ethical appeal can still be accomplished, but it needs to be delivered by another speaker, preferably someone the audience already knows and whom they believe to be knowledgeable and honest and well-meaning. This is, in fact, the only reason for any speaker-controlled introduction—to tell the audience why they should listen to the speaker.

While any of these tactics by itself might seem futile, their combined effect is substantial. Imagine if Arthur Anderson had held a press conference as soon as it was implicated in the ENRON scandal. Their speaker interviewee is introduced by a trusted member of the international business community. The Arthur Anderson spokesperson next acknowledges the company's mishandling of ENRON, divulges an internal probe that revealed similar activities, and outlines a plan to purge unethical and illegal practices and put the organization back on its feet. Of course, this example is a fairy tale because Arthur Anderson never showed it had the wisdom or the courage to meet the issue head on, but consider what might have happened if it had.

Chapter Seven

Probing—The Employment or Behavior Interview

The employment interview is the model for the behavior interview. The behavior interview is the second of two categories of probing interviews, the first being journalistic. In both cases interviewers gather data and observe behavior, but the behavior-based interviewer seeks mainly to study the interviewee, while the journalistic interviewer is concerned with finding out what the interviewee knows about a topic. Journalistic interviews are discussed in the previous chapter. This chapter will focus on the employment interview. By learning to conduct the employment interview, students of interviewing will have acquired a base of knowledge and skills that will help them adapt to other specialized forms of behavior interviewing like those used in counseling and human behavior research.

The employment interview is by far the most frequently occurring form of behavior interview. Almost everyone of high school age or older has participated in a job interview. There are also hundreds of printed and online resources with information and statistics on job interviews. Unfortunately most job interviews are mishandled, and a good deal of what we have learned through experience needs to be unlearned. Much of the literature on employment interviews needs to be set aside as well, as it focuses on formulas and scripted questions and responses. The most effective employment interview is a process that involves probing for evidence of behavior. Those who understand the behavior probing process have a significant advantage over interviewees and interviewers who do not.

While interviewing by definition is results-oriented, the reason for conducting an employment interview is often misunderstood. Most people would say one conducts a job interview in order to hire someone, but this is not true. People are hired without being tested by job interviews every day. No, an interview is not a requirement for hiring. What the interview

lends the hiring process is a degree of predictability. ***The behavior-based
employment interview is used to predict a job applicant's compatibility
and performance in a particular business culture.***

The Rhetoric of Behavior

Employment and other behavior interviews are not so concerned with
what someone does as with the *pattern* of what someone does—with his
or her behavior. There are three broad categories of behavior theories. A
faith-based understanding of behavior attributes our actions to mostly in-
discernible forces that impact our lives either because we have petitioned
them or because we are unable to resist them. Another broad category
finds the engine of human activity in the tension between randomness and
human will. The third, behaviorism, holds that behavior is due mainly to
observation and conditioning and that humans have little choice but to
play out the trajectories of past experience. Proponents might argue they
are mutually exclusive, but who has lived and has not seen evidence of
each of these paradigms? The behavior-based employment interview falls
clearly in the third category. It necessarily seeks to learn about past and
present behavior in order to predict future behavior. Without an understanding that behaviorism at least plays a role in human activity, there is
no reason to conduct an employment interview.

Aristotle writes that only science and philosophy deal with things that
can be known. Rhetoric is the discourse of what we cannot know. By definition then, the category of what we do not know, rhetoric, is infinitely
larger than the category of what we do know, science and philosophy. Yet,
while the category of rhetorical discourse is larger, its footprint is smaller.
For Aristotle, science deals with the physical universe, and philosophy
with the rational universe, but rhetoric has as its domain the unwritten
script of human experience. We know the laws of science because they can
be proven through experimentation, and we know the truths of philosophy
because they stand the test of logic, but there are no absolutes to be measured or reasoned in the human drama. Here we are limited to assessing
probabilities, tendencies, and potentiality. The weight of gold, the square
root of nine will always be the same, but observations of human behavior
are reifications—seemingly solid and predictable calms and gusts and cy-
clones on a stage that by any scientific measure would be empty.

One might conclude that the behavior interview is a useless tool. It
looks for behavior which may or may not predict how people will act in
the future, and it classifies it with the language of reification, which ap-
proximates things that do not exist. It is true, yet therein lies its value. The
behavior interview may be useless. It may be misleading. And it may turn

chaos into order. Other than by observing someone's life, there is no better way to access the pattern of his or her behavior. We know that sometimes people change when they accept or reject God or when they acquire or lose mental discipline, but most people, most of the time, play out the patterns formed by past experience. As we use rhetorical discourse because it is our best method to guide our steps into the uncertainty of economic policy and military action, so to we use rhetorical discourse to guide us through the uncertainty of counseling the bereaved, committing to marriage, and assembling a workforce. We can never know these things with certainty, but this is how we make our best guess.

The Typical Hiring Process

Hiring does not begin and end with an interview. It is an ongoing process. A good hiring process starts with developing or revising a job description. The job description can then be used to write a job posting and a classified newspaper ad. As letters of application and resumes come in, they are reviewed and categorized. Then the top candidates are screened and called in for interviews. An interview guide is written and the interviews are conducted. A candidate is selected, an offer is made, and a contract is negotiated. Then the new hire attends an employee orientation. Six months later, and every six months after that, the employee goes through a review process. The employee may migrate to other jobs within the organization or may choose to leave. When the employee announces he or she is leaving, there is an exit interview in which the job description is reviewed, and the process starts over.

Most companies do not see the value of all these steps in the hiring process. They may hire new employees without any of the pre-hiring steps and throw the new person on the job without taking any of the post-hiring steps. In worst-case-scenario companies, the employee never participates in a review process and may not even be sure who he or she reports to. Typically, companies that spend no time on the hiring process hire the wrong people for the job and leave them in place for years before realizing their mistake. This creates problems, which are resolved by announcing layoffs and firing the employees who are so mismatched and dysfunctional that it has become apparent even in a system with little capacity to monitor its workforce.

The Ideal Hiring Process

Most of the bad practices in American business can be traced to the Great Depression and World War II in the 20th Century. Reckless profiteering by big business in the 1920s drove the nation into economic collapse by the end of the decade. The unemployment rate was 25 percent when Franklin Roosevelt took office in 1932. At that time the workforce was almost entirely men. By today's standards, where women make up half of the workforce, the equivalent unemployment rate would be over 60 percent. Understandably, people who had jobs did whatever they had to do to keep them. The economic depression of the 1930s was followed by the war effort in the 1940s. Workers at home made sacrifices while their brothers and sisters in arms learned to give and take orders in the wartime military. It is easy to see how the human side of the employment equation was ignored under these circumstances. Unfortunately, the business culture of the 1930s and 1940s carried over to the 1950s and 1960s, while American businesses were expanding and becoming more dependent on middle management. By the 1970s America was experiencing a quality crisis. It was particularly apparent in the steel and auto industries.

Old habits die hard. Consumer groups, management consultants, and innovative business leaders began a revolution in American businesses in the 1970s by calling attention to the problems: decision-making was too far removed from the frontline employee and the customer, employees felt alienated from organizational goals, and middle managers had built up fiefdoms where they played favorites, harassed women and minorities, and ignored their leadership responsibilities. Some companies, some industries, and even some areas of the country responded to the call for change. But most business leaders and managers saw the changes as meaningless buzzwords and political correctness. While the majority of the 21st century workforce never experienced the dark ages of business culture in the mid 20th century, many of their bosses and company presidents did and its influence is still with us.

From a communication perspective, the problematic business system is closed, the desirable system is open. In a closed system information only passes from the top of the organization down, and it is usually inadequate and infrequent. In an open system information flow is driven by information need, and it moves up the chain of command as easily as it moves down. Closed systems resist change and are slow to recognize and mend problems. Open systems are constantly anticipating and adapting to change.

Closed system companies that want to become open should start with the hiring process. The quality of the workforce, its motivation, and its ability to perform are all linked to the process that selects, trains, and empowers employees. The ideal hiring process is one where employees hire their coworkers, and where managers are leaders and mentors who facilitate the process. When someone announces he or she is leaving, an ad hoc committee is formed. The committee is made up of coworkers who will be peers and perhaps subordinates of the person filling the open position.

They perform the exit interview and review and redesign the job description. Next they place an ad and review applications. They screen the best applicants over the phone and through record checks. Then they conduct a determinate interview with the most qualified candidates and gauge who will perform best in the business culture. When the committee is finished, they send two candidates to the supervisor. The supervisor then interviews each candidate and selects one.

This entire process is facilitated by the supervisor with the assistance of human resources. The committee of coworkers develops the job description because they know the job better than their managers. They also have to work with the new employee, so they are the ones most motivated to make a good choice. Because the manager is concerned with results rather than with control, he or she lets the people closest to the job select the top candidates. The manager makes the final choice because the manager is ultimately accountable for the quality of the work done by the new employee. By the time the hire is made, everyone in the work group is invested in the process, and there is a high probability that the right candidate will be hired and will successfully adapt to the culture.

This is not what most of us are used to. In many companies, supervisors perform all the steps in the hiring process, or worse, human resources does it for them. Even when the process is executed by committee, exit interviews are rare and job descriptions may be nonexistent, irrelevant, or just ignored. Records go unchecked as well. In 2001 the University of Notre Dame asked for the resignation of its new football coach five days after they had hired him. They learned through newspaper reports that the master's degree and college football career reported on his resume were bogus.

One common misstep is that instead of sending for records and scrutinizing references, companies perform a useless screening interview. There is no need for a screening interview to check credentials; even the most experienced interviewer will have trouble getting job applicants to admit to lying on their resumes or volunteer that they are late for work on a regular basis. The committee can select several leading candidates, check their references, and verify their credentials all before anyone is called in for a meeting. Not only is this more effective, it is also more efficient. The hiring process is time consuming, and as much time as possible needs to be reserved for the determinate interview where qualified candidates are scrutinized to discover which one will best fit in the business culture. The task of studying someone's behavior is interview dependent; the other steps are not.

The problems that occur when human resources departments do the hiring have nothing to do with negligence; they are systemic. The staff in human resources necessarily works with generic hiring criteria and with vague and usually outdated job descriptions. Worst of all, human resources has no real accountability. If the new employee is incompetent, the coworkers and supervisor in the department will suffer every day, and human resources may never know about it. The coworker committee on the other hand is similar to a quality circle. A quality circle is a group of employees who are internal customers of one another. They meet and redesign their jobs to better meet their combined needs. A good workgroup-based hiring process incorporates this key principle of employee participation and eliminates the need for periodic quality campaigns to readjust the business culture. The personnel department performs best as a resource for the committee. They can monitor the hiring process, provide interview training, and consult on policy issues for the ad hoc workgroup committee.

The Employment Interview Guide

Work on the employment interview guide begins with the job description. There is no better time to review a job description than when someone is leaving a position. The exit interview can provide up-to-the-minute insights on the job from the person who knows it best. Essentially, the job description is a list of competencies and qualities, and, if it were used as a guide for the interview, it would be more effective than the random lists of questions employed by most interviewers. However, since the greatest value of the probing interview is to explore behavior, it is most useful to convert the job description into a list of behaviors.

Some behaviors are valuable in almost all jobs, and others are job specific. The almost universally desirable employee behaviors are

Adaptable	Knowledgeable	Resourceful
Articulate	Organized	Results-oriented
Collegial	Personable	Self-motivated
Honest	Professional	Strategic

Other behaviors are more job specific:

Aggressive	Discerning	Nurturing
Ambitious	Disciplined	Patient
Analytical	Empathic	Persistent
Assertive	Enduring	Persuasive
Cautious	Energetic	Resilient
Compassionate	Entrepreneurial	Responsible
Competitive	Independent	Risk-taking

Consistent	Innovative	Self-confident
Courageous	Inquisitive	Sensitive
Decisive	Insightful	Strong-willed
Dependable	Flexible	Team-oriented
Detail-oriented	Frugal	Tenacious
Diligent	Mentoring	Visionary

Some of these behaviors are overlapping and others are contradictory. A hiring committee looking for an insurance investigator would value inquisitiveness, a committee hiring a mail carrier might find the behavior problematic, whereas everyone wants to hire someone who is results-oriented. No job would call for all of these behaviors, and certainly no job applicant is capable of exhibiting all of them. At best, a company might select a few necessary behaviors, and a few more desirable behaviors. Candidates would be interviewed and discussed, and an offer would be made to the person who represented the best available match.

Each of these items represents not just a skill, but a potential habit or pattern of behavior. The difference between skill and behavior is significant. Most professionals have organizational skills, but not everyone has the self-discipline to organize his or her affairs. Certainly people who have never practiced organizational skills can learn to do so, but would you rather hire employees who have learned organizational skills and are organized, or employees who may have learned them and might become organized if you force them? A little time and effort spent probing behavior can save hundreds of hours correcting behavior.

In October, 2005, the Tuscaloosa News ran an ad for a general assignment reporter. They said that they had a circulation of 38,000 and that they annually swept the awards in Alabama newspaper contests. Their ideal job candidate had to be "hard-working," have a "creative flair," and be able to write enterprise stories from routine daily news. They also wanted someone who could "report with fresh eyes a region steeped in tradition." The candidate needed some experience, but had to be willing to learn. He or she would be given one of the most important beats at the newspaper. It ended by asking applicants to contact Anna Maria Della Costa, the city editor. Obviously a great deal of thought went into this ad. Can you identify the behavior requirements? Here are some of the behaviors you might have discovered in the order in which they appeared:

Competitiveness	Professionalism	Adaptability
Diligence	Inquisitiveness	
Creativity	Discernment	

Most of the work for developing the guide is completed by the time a search committee has identified behaviors and written the classified ad. The interviewer mainly utilizes the rhetorical canon of arrangement to turn the behaviors into the guide. A guide for Anna Marie Della Costa and her committee at *The Tuscaloosa News* might look like this:

1. Creativity
2. Inquisitiveness
3. Discernment
4. Professionalism
5. Diligence
6. Adaptability
7. Competitiveness

Creativity and inquisitiveness are first because they meet the requirement of beginning with an easy, enjoyable conversation. Almost everyone who is a writer believes he or she is creative, and anyone who wants to become a reporter had better be inquisitive. Inquisitiveness serves two purposes: it is easy to talk about for a reporter, and it serves as a bridge to a more difficult behavior, discernment. Remember, conducting an interview is like taking the interviewee for a walk through interior space. The interviewer benefits when one topic leads to another, particularly if the second topic resides at a deeper, more meaningful level. Anyone can be inquisitive, but discernment refers to what we do with our inquisitiveness. Without scripting the questions, the interviewer knows he or she can probably get the interviewee to discuss being inquisitive and probe into a discussion of discernment without changing the subject and starting over.

Professionalism is next because it is a broad issue. The interviewer can draw on information revealed in the preceding discussions of creativity, inquisitiveness, and discernment. If professionalism is too early in the interview it will probably be discussed in the abstract, like a generic dictionary definition. Placed as it is in the middle, it allows the interviewer to cite specific circumstances and opinions stated earlier by the interviewee and get a more personal and revealing response. Perhaps the interviewee mentioned sneaking into a retirement home to investigate a tip about the mistreatment of residents as an example of inquisitiveness. Later, under the heading of professionalism, the interviewer can cite the nursing home investigation and ask the interviewee to discuss it in terms of professionalism with questions like: why didn't you announce yourself and go through channels? The interviewer may feel the interviewee was justified in going undercover but still probe the incident to learn to what extent the interviewee considered and was constrained by professional ethics.

Anyone can claim to be diligent and adaptable. These guide items are placed next because discussing professionalism will have a sobering effect on the conversation. It is most likely that the interviewee will give careful, thoughtful answers after having been made accountable during the professionalism discussion. Also, at this point the interviewer and interviewee should have established a degree of trust and mutual respect, and the interview can safely move to the other side of the emotional spectrum—from the easy, fun topics of creativity and inquisitiveness, to deeper psychological territory of diligence and adaptability. Diligence implies sacrificing what one wants to do for what one needs to do, and adaptability usually means setting aside familiarity and pride and embracing change. If all has gone well, it should be possible for the interviewer to get the interviewee to provide examples of past behavior that can be probed to reveal the interviewee's thought process and priorities regarding these two behaviors.

Competitiveness is last because the discussion of competitiveness will benefit most from all that has preceded it. Competitiveness is also somewhat parallel with creativity. It is potentially a more fun topic like creativity than a soul-searching topic like professionalism, diligence, and adaptability. When competitiveness has been exhausted, the interviewer can ask a clearinghouse probe, thank the interviewee, and close the interview.

Behavior Probing

Effective behavior probing requires a degree of subtlety. If the guide item is "honesty," the interviewer can't just ask the interviewee, "are you honest." An honest person would answer yes, and a dishonest person would, of course, also answer yes. To get the best information about behavior, an interviewer has to construct a two tiered discussion. On one level the interview is focused on a real or hypothetical experience, and on another level the interview is focused on the behavior that is revealed by that experience. Interviewees, particularly job applicants, are usually prepared to tell the interviewer whatever they think he or she wants to hear. This means the interviewer cannot ask the interviewee about the behavior directly. The discussion needs to be developed in such a way that the interviewee does not guess what behavior the interviewer is looking for.

If you want to explore leadership, do not say, "tell me about a time when you exercised good leadership." The question needs to be more neutral: "tell me about an experience with a group project that went poorly."

From there the interviewer can probe the experience and gauge the extent to which the interviewee understands and is able to explain problems in terms of leadership, and in many cases, explore how the interviewee responded to the problem by exercising or not exercising leadership. When the subject is exhausted, then and only then can the interviewer be direct: "how would you evaluate your team in terms of leadership?"

An interviewer who asks about behavior in the wrong way would be better off if he or she had not conducted a behavior interview at all. A common mistake is for the interviewer to tell the interviewee what behaviors the company is looking for before asking the question! The naïve interviewer sees "compassion" on the guide and says to the interviewee: "Ours is a caring hospital, we are looking for nurses with compassion. Are you compassionate?" Almost everyone has had moments of compassion, and most people probably want to believe they are compassionate. So, if your screening process has filtered out the sociopaths, the chances of getting a yes answer here are 100 percent. Another problem with this compassion example is that it is closed. The question might seem more effective if it were open: "Compassion is very important for us here at Silver Cross Hospital; what does compassion mean to you?" Or: ". . . give me an example of a time where you showed compassion." Is this slightly better? Yes, interviewees will give interviewers more information answering open questions, but they still know what the interviewers are looking for. Thus, the answers probably will be even more beguiling. Regrettably, interviewers who telegraph what they are looking for come away with false impressions, and false impressions are worse than no impressions at all.

Accounting

The key to effective probing is accounting. Accounting questions ask an interviewee to justify an action or a comment. Accounting questions can follow almost any interviewee comment. If the interviewee says, "I didn't finish school because my job was too demanding of my time," the interviewer can follow with, "why was your job more important than your education?" If the interviewee says, "I never really thought about why I quit school, I just didn't go back one year," the interviewer can ask, "why didn't you think about it?" If the interviewee says, "I don't want to talk about this," the interviewer can ask, "why don't you want to talk about it?"

Accounting is a kind of universal stasis point for behavior interviews. Whatever direction an interview goes in, a question that asks an interviewee to explain a choice, an action, a reason, or even a word almost always drives the discussion into deeper revelations of behavior. This technique is so powerful that the interviewee may be as surprised by his or her answers as the interviewer is.

Probing Sequences

Probing is more effective as part of a long sequence. An answer to a primary question should be followed with a question that probes the answer to the first question, not with the next primary question. The third question should be one that probes the answer to the second question. The fourth question should probe the answer to the third question and so on. An entire interview could take place off of only one primary question.

Two techniques make a long meaningful string of probing possible. One is ask only open questions, and the other is ask accounting questions. The human psyche is infinitely complex. When open accounting questions are asked in an unbroken series, they drive deeper and deeper into the interior landscape. The skill of asking open accounting questions can be developed to the point where it is routine. Then the interviewer becomes less concerned with how to keep the string of questions alive and more concerned with evaluating the usefulness of the responses. At some point the interviewee may begin to reveal information that is not useful or appropriate. Then the interviewer needs to express appreciation for the interviewee's cooperation, ask a closed question, and move to the next item on the guide.

Leveraged Questions

A leveraged question is one where the interviewer already knows or will soon know the answer, and the interviewee is forced to reveal information that might otherwise have been left unsaid. For instance, if the hiring process requires applicants to submit college transcripts, but they have not arrived prior to the interview, the interviewer can say to the interviewee, "Your transcripts have not arrived yet; can you tell me what your approximate grade point average was?" An intelligent interviewee, even one who is not compelled to be honest, knows that he or she has to supply the correct answer. A quick survey of options and consequences reveals why. If the GPA is a good one, then there is no reason not to announce it. If it is poor and the interviewee lies and reports a higher number, the interviewer will soon find out the real number and conclude that the interviewee is dishonest. Companies often take chances on applicants who didn't perform well in school, but rarely will they take a chance on someone they know to be dishonest. Not answering, or claiming not to remember are problematic as well. If the GPA is low, the interviewee is better off saying so in the interview where he or she can mitigate its impact.

The effect is lost if there has been no request for transcripts. And the effect is greatly lessened if the interviewer says, "we might require that you have your transcripts sent." However, the worst application of the leveraged question is when the interviewer claims to know something, or promises to check something, but has no intention to do so. All of these variations of the leveraged question are undesirable, but the last is unethical. Interviewees are looking for indications of what the business culture might be like, and an interviewer lying in order to be manipulative is a strong indication of an undesirable theory X culture. An interviewer who wants to use the leveraged question must resolve always to require transcripts, contact the former supervisor, call references, or do whatever he or she is claiming to do in the leveraged question. Announced intentions can be skipped only if the interviewee's answer causes the interviewee to be eliminated from consideration.

Don't Accept Generalities

A common rhetorical mechanism is to speak in pleasant generalities. That is, when we could give a specific answer, we give a safer, non-specific one instead. For instance: "How are you?" usually gets the response, "I'm fine." This kind of unfocused conversation is acceptable if not mandatory in casual, nonprofessional interactions, but it is unacceptable in an employment interview. If the interviewer asks, "What do you like most about your current job?" the expectation is that the interviewee will give a specific answer like, "It's so rewarding to work with children." The interviewer can then say "Define rewarding for me," and the probing begins. But if the first answer is "I've liked all my jobs, I just love to work," the interviewee has effectively shut down the interview. The interviewer needs to take this as a serious challenge and let the interviewee know the answer is not acceptable. Instead of moving to the next item on the guide, the interviewer needs to say something like "I want to know something specific that you like about your current job." This second question should be polite, but said with the understanding that both parties know the interviewer is exercising his or her authority. Some interviewees have a problem engaging in specific conversation, and it may be necessary for the interviewer to restate more than one question to get the interview on track.

Questions are Context Dependent

There is no such thing as a good question. The effectiveness of a question in drawing out meaningful information is entirely dependent on the interviewee and the rhetorical situation. One interviewee might easily volunteer that he or she thrives on competition, another might only arrive at that conclusion after a long, arduous probing sequence. Interviewers who think they can conduct an interview using a schedule of sure-fire questions downloaded from the internet or copied from an interviewing book are mistaken. The most evocative, reliable information is uncovered because of the interviewer's skills, not from a clever list of questions.

Don't Be a Cheerleader

The cheerleader interviewer nods in agreement with every answer, self-discloses agreement, and even compliments the interviewee on how well he or she is performing. Cheerleading is a seductive communication habit. The interviewer wants to build rapport, and the interviewee wants approval. Both parties are emotionally geared up to look for and capitalize on bonding opportunities, and the employment interview provides them with every question and every answer. Nodding and smiling with approval while an interviewee is answering a question is like throwing gasoline on a fire. Unfortunately, rapport between a job applicant and a job interviewer is worthless unless it contributes to the collection of meaningful insights about behavior. The interviewer should distribute approval like a doctor prescribing narcotics. There is need for showing compassion, expressing approval, or even initiating some bonding interaction early in the interview. Interviewees will be asked some difficult questions as the interview progresses, and it is good if they know they are talking to a compassionate human being and not an automaton focused only on recording their mistakes. Once the interview begins in earnest, however, the interviewer needs only express approval or engage in self-disclosure if the interviewee has finished a particularly difficult series of answers. The only other exception is the close of the interview when the interviewer is expressing appreciation.

Bidirectional Interviewing

The purpose of the employment interview is not to hire the applicant. It is to look for evidence of behavior to decide to hire, or not to hire, the applicant. This means that negative information is as valuable as positive information.

If it becomes increasingly apparent that the candidate is undesirable, the interviewer may need to switch from probing positive issues to probing negative ones. If, in an interview for a prison guard, the interviewee reveals an authority complex and a tendency toward cruelty and violence, it would be silly to proceed with guide items asking about balancing compassion and keeping order. If the interviewer believes he or she has found a reason not to hire the applicant, then it may be best to spend a significant portion of the interview testing the negative observation. Bidirectional means the interview can go in two directions. Consider the interview as a proposition: this candidate should be hired by our company. By the time the interview is finished, the interviewer will have proved it or disproved it.

Equal Employment Opportunity Laws and Guidelines

Equal employment opportunity or EEO laws and guidelines protect our rights to seek employment and be treated fairly on the job. In principle, EEO laws and guidelines prohibit employers from discriminating against job applicants for reasons of race, gender, or age. These regulations benefit everyone, even the companies and managers who sometimes complain about them. The rights protected by EEO are guaranteed throughout the U.S. Constitution, its amendments, and many federal and state laws that delineate the privileges of citizenship. Sometimes managers feel that these regulations interfere with their rights to hire and fire whomever they please, but EEO reminds us that voting and other privileges are of little consequence if we are denied the right to make a living. Citizens who feel their rights have been violated can bring suit against employers who, if they are found guilty, could have to pay fines and reimburse claimants for lost wages. Thus, it is with the fear of monetary penalties that the state forces reluctant employers to comply.

Most of the rights covered by EEO are already guaranteed through the Constitution, the amendments, and other laws. However, it was not until the 1960s that EEO began to be articulated and enforced. Prior to EEO, it was not uncommon for companies and even schools to have policies forbidding the hiring of African Americans, Jews, Greeks, Irish, Italians, Mexicans, or anyone who seemed foreign at the time. Women were often limited to roles as secretaries and file clerks and routinely had to put up with sexual advances and demeaning comments from male coworkers. There are those who argue that EEO represents government interference in the marketplace, but there is probably no better example of a failure of the free market philosophy and the need for government intervention than the positive changes brought about in the workplace through EEO.

Following EEO laws and guidelines is fairly simple. Do not deny a job opportunity to anyone because of race, gender, or age. The only criteria for filtering candidates out of the process should be what is listed in the job description. When conducting the interview, ask only job related questions. And don't ask questions that you would not ask of all applicants. Applying EEO hardly requires a law degree; common sense will do.

Assessing the Applicant

There are three ways to assess the interviewee: through past behavior, with hypothetical situations, and observation of behavior during the interview itself. None of this will produce hard evidence, but an astute interviewer will, in most cases, come away with enough information to know if a particular interviewee is worth the risk of a job offer. Past experience is to be preferred over hypothetical scenarios. Putting interviewees into hypothetical situations has some limited uses, but most interviewees can shape hypothetical answers to meet the expectations of interviewers. Someone hired based on answers to hypothetical questions was really hired for his or her imagination and verbal skills. A somewhat more reliable predictor of future behavior is past behavior. Asking an interviewee what he or she did, followed by a series of probing questions will, in most cases, give the interviewer a good idea of what to expect if the person is hired. Of course, anyone can make up answers, but few interviewees will be able to put together a long string of credible answers to a series of probing follow-up questions.

Observing behavior during the interview will provide the best insights in most cases. If, for instance, the interviewer is looking for assertiveness, the behavior should show up throughout the interview. However, it is not recommended that the interviewer stage opportunities to test behavior by trying to get the interviewee upset, or pretending to be offended, or using any other dramatic ploy. The interview is necessarily dependent on a level of trust between the interviewer and interviewee. Staging insincere interactions to test behavior is unethical and counterproductive.

Once a behavior topic has been explored and observed, and if the interviewer has observed a discrepancy between the interviewee's accounts and the interviewee's actions, it is not inappropriate to ask for an explanation. If the interviewee claims to be self-motivated, but has shown no evidence of self-motivation during the interview, the interviewer may ask why. Rather than being offended, an astute interviewee will see this as an opportunity to address an important issue. Listening to and probing the response should provide significant insight into the issue.

Closing the Employment Interview

If the interview has gone well, a degree of mutual respect and friendship will have developed. The interviewer knows that the interviewee is looking for affirmation and some hint as to how well he or she performed. The interviewer needs to resist the temptation to respond to this. Keep the focus on the interview, not the job. Thank the interviewee for cooperating, and if necessary provide a brief orientation of the remaining steps of the hiring process.

Chapter Eight

The Interviewee in the Employment Interview

The Job Search Process

Hiring is a process, and so is getting hired. A job applicant identifies an employment goal and begins looking for opportunities, resumes and cover letters are sent, and interviews are scheduled. The search phase continues until a position is accepted. Simultaneously with the search, there is ongoing preparation for the job interview. An aggressive job applicant identifies his or her strengths and weaknesses and develops an interviewee's interview guide around the strengths. Each successive job interview, whether or not it nets an offer, is an opportunity to practice with the guide. Eventually an offer is received and the active job search is over. After taking the position, one makes new business contacts, develops new skills, and establishes a reputation, all which engender promotions, future job offers, and references.

The old adage that 100 resumes sent nets 5 to 10 interviews and one job offer still holds true. Students who graduate in June and immediately mail out 100 resumes usually have jobs by July or August. Students who take a year to get out the first 100 resumes usually take a year to find a job.

Another aspect of the hiring process is that it is seasonal. Holidays and budget transitions make hiring difficult for almost half of the year. Hiring in certain fields is also affected by swings in the economy. Most fields put hiring on hold during an economic downturn, but that doesn't mean you should stop looking for a job. In some fields an economic slowdown has the opposite effect. And even companies that are laying off workers still have job vacancies that they have to fill.

The job search process has one other thing in common with the hiring process: it is ongoing. Whether or not you intend to look for a new job, as a professional you are constantly building a reputation and a network of contacts. Many professionals find that the only job they actively looked for was the first one. All the other jobs came from unexpected offers from business contacts. Every day at work provides opportunities for new contacts and new references and for generating new experience and proficiencies. The accumulation of work and life experience is the substance of the next resume and the subject of the next job interview.

Who Are You and What Do You Want?

Without honest self-assessment, the job candidate has no more control over his or her fate than a gambler at a roulette wheel. Some people think they can do anything. Some feel they are inferior and incompetent. Others have never given it much thought and find the gambling metaphor to be quite acceptable. If you fall into one of these categories, books and classes on employment interviews will be of little use to you. If you want to exercise some control over your fate, start by realizing that no one is perfect, and no one is totally useless. Self-assessment doesn't require that people benchmark themselves against the best professionals in their fields, just that they consider their own strengths and weaknesses and identify what they do best. It is true that there is an element of chance in every human endeavor, but a wise job applicant studies his or her own strengths and strategizes to maximize their impact and minimize the role of chance.

Self-assessment for the job search process doesn't require psychoanalysis. One either does or does not have certain kinds of experience, skills, and behaviors. Make your list. What are your academic credentials? What have you learned on the job? What do you do well, and with what can you say you have familiarity from experience? Don't try to make the list all at once. Start a list and carry it around for a few days. Show it to people you trust and ask them for feedback. Consider the list of behaviors from the employment interview chapter. Select the behaviors that most apply to you. Show this list to friends and coworkers. Be ready for some surprises. If your current work experience hasn't provided opportunities for honest feedback, you will probably find that some of what you think are your strengths are perceived as weaknesses and some of what you think are weaknesses are really strengths. The assessment phase is invaluable in preparing a resume and an interviewee's interview guide. It may also cause one not to look for a new position, or to consider a career change.

The Marketing Model

Marketing strategies are increasingly overvalued and overused. The larger the public, the more problematic it becomes to generalize about wants and needs. But marketing is an ideal way to approach the job search process.

In most professions, job requirements are fairly consistent from company to company. For attorneys, accountants, professors, medical doctors, even managers, there are skills and behaviors that are universally desirable. This means that as a job candidate, your customers are fairly predictable. Your product is also predictable because it is you. If you know what you have to offer, and you know what your customers are looking for, it isn't too difficult to anticipate what you need to put in a resume and say in a job interview.

There are several ways to assess the needs of potential employers. If you are currently in the field, study the list of employee behaviors and select the behaviors that the ideal professional would possess. Also, look at want ads in your area. What are the ads asking for? Personal observations and advertising are both good places to start, but the best source of information is in job interviews themselves. Consider each interview not just as an opportunity to get a job, but an opportunity to learn about employers. Combining the behaviors you believe are essential with the behaviors listed in the ads and the behaviors most frequently raised in ongoing interviews will yield a step-by-step tracking system for your target public.

Another valuable lesson from marketing and advertising research is that people can easily be overwhelmed with too much information. This means that when you prepare your interviewing guide, you limit yourself to no more than three key items and that you repeat them as often as possible. This may sound silly, but remember, the interviewer will ostensibly have control of the interview. You are slipping your points in when the opportunities arise. If this is done right, the interviewer will take credit for discovering your three key behaviors.

When one considers that most employment interviewers and interviewees are unprepared, the results of an interviewee-managed interview can be profound. If the interviewer had no guide and you managed to repeat your three key behaviors three times each, chances are the interviewer will still have them on his or her mind when conducting successive interviews. You actually steer not only your own interview into advantageous territory, but all of the subsequent interviews as well. The hiring decision may be made by comparing all the candidates to your three strengths.

Identifying Key Behaviors

Selecting three behaviors as selling points is the pivotal strategy in the job search process. For most people, it may be as simple as making a list of desirable behaviors based on what you know about the job and comparing it to a list of your own most established behaviors. Stack rank the two lists from most desirable to least desirable behaviors and select the top three matches.

If the job is in public relations, then a specialized list of most desired behaviors for a professional probably includes high ethical standards, writing interests and talent, a valuing and respect of opinion research, creativity, preciseness, a serious commitment to prioritizing and time-management, comfort and versatility with general communication, self-motivation, leadership, and familiarity with and interest in computer based layout and design. Note that this is a list of behaviors, not skills. Skills can be checked prior to the determinant interview. Anyone who has not taken a news writing class will not be called in for an interview for a professional public relations job. The final decision for hiring will be made among several candidates who have the same skills, thus making behavior the crucial issue. If all candidates can write news style, then the candidate who most demonstrates behaviors like creativity, accuracy, and a love of meeting people and conducting interviews will get the job.

The list of personal behaviors is more difficult to generate than the list of desirable behaviors because it requires supporting evidence. It isn't enough to just say "Yes, I think I can do that," or even, "I really like to write." It would be good to develop one or more items for your personal behavior list that can apply to writing. It may be creativity, or an ability to work alone for long hours, or an appreciation for feedback. Thus the candidate would put "love of hearing from readers" on the interviewee guide. During the interview, the interviewer says, "I see you worked on the school newspaper, took three news writing courses, and an English course on poetry; tell me about your writing." The prepared interviewee responds with: "I love writing because I love the interaction with my readers." After discussing this, the interviewer will come away knowing that you cannot only write, but you like to write. And the interviewer will trust the information because it is true and you were able to support it by talking about it in depth. Note, the interviewee guide is to be reviewed before the interview begins, not during the interview.

The selection of personal behaviors for the interviewee guide cannot be a matter of wishful thinking. Each item selected should have supporting material, preferably stories that punctuate your behavior claim. Suppose the public relations job applicant selects leadership. Leadership is low on the ideal applicant list but is included because it is high on the applicant's personal list, and the job applicant has much to say about it. The interviewer may ask, "How would you coordinate a project like putting out an annual report?" Potentially one could talk about behaviors like being results oriented or having high standards, and one could talk about leadership. Leadership is on the interviewee guide, so the interviewee responds: "This is essentially a leadership responsibility, and I see leadership more as facilitating than telling people what to do. When I was features editor at *The Chronicle*, I asked my writers to submit story ideas . . ."

The interviewee's guide should have no more than three behaviors listed. As subcategories under each behavior are references to stories that can be told to make a point about the behavior. The public relations job applicant above would have a list that looks like this:

Love of interaction with readers
- Response to editorial on parking garage
- Rewarding relationship with journalism instructor
- Participation in writer's workshop

Leadership
- Developing writers at student newspaper
- Observations on speech class project that bombed
- Successful organization of students on survey project

Self-motivated
- Volunteer publicity work at local animal shelter
- Graduating from college without family support
- Redesign of student newspaper features section

Practicing for the Interview

One prepares for the interview mainly by practicing telling stories. Put each of the three behaviors on an index card. Underneath each heading, write key words to remind yourself of the story that serves as evidence of the behavior. Carry the cards with you and look at them whenever you get a chance. Maybe you are on the train to Boston for an interview. Review your cards. Read the behavior, and then put the card down. Can you recall the stories? Now look at a story heading, put the card down, and tell yourself the story. The point isn't to memorize your stories word for word, just to remember the details and become fluent in telling them. It would be counterproductive if it sounded like you were reciting during the interview. The more you review your material, the more comfortable you will be adapting it to questions in a live interview. As you review your material, other stories may come to mind. Add them to the list. Three behaviors is a maximum number because they need to be repeated and reinforced, and it is unlikely an interviewer will retain more than three. However, the stories that support the behaviors have no such restriction. They can only be told once each, and it is impossible to predict which ones will best fit into the interview. Therefore, the more stories you have the better.

Discussing behaviors and telling stories is not as difficult as it might sound. The behaviors are actual behaviors that you have exhibited in the past, not behaviors that you made up just to impress the interviewer. And the stories are actual experiences. Do not be tempted to fabricate or garnish them. Honesty is the tacit behavior requirement in all interviews. Being honest will make a better impression than exaggerating your experiences, and it will also make it much easier for you to remember what to say.

Another way to get additional practice is give your interviewee interview guide to a friend and ask him or her to interview you. There is no substitute for live interview experience, however. The best practice is the job interview itself. Interviewees will get better with each experience. For this reason, it is a good policy to go to every job interview opportunity that presents itself, even if you don't think you are interested in the job. If you get an offer you don't want, you can always say no. Perhaps at a future interview there will be an opportunity to mention that you were offered a job by another company and turned it down. Letting the interviewer know that someone else offered you a job has a similar psychological effect as a positive character reference.

Answering Questions in the Interview

Whether or not interviewers are prepared, they think they are in charge of the interview, and interviewees should do nothing to cause them to feel like they have lost control. For an interviewer, the ideal interviewee trait is cooperativeness. The more interviewers sense cooperation, the more they drop their guard, and the easier it becomes for interviewees to insert their own agendas. If interviewers feel like they are sparring in a verbal contest, they will exercise greater control and treat interviewee comments with skepticism.

Job interviews should last from one to two hours, so there is no need for an interviewee to become anxious and pushy. Spend the first ten minutes of the interview responding as directly and fully as possible to interviewer questions. Then test the waters by inserting a behavior story. Most interviewers will be grateful that the interviewee has opened up. They will be patient and may encourage you to tell them more. When you are done, return control of the interview to the interviewer and wait for your next opportunity. If the interviewer seems impatient when you tell your behavior story and changes the subject when you are done, then you need to make accommodations for an unusually defensive interview environment. Instead of telling stories, try dropping tidbits of interesting information. Chances are the interviewer will be intrigued by something and ask you to elaborate. If possible, try to tell the story in pieces, requiring the interviewer to ask you to tell more. The rare interviewer who conducts the interview like a highly scheduled survey will have an extremely limited pool of information from which to analyze job candidates, thus leaving the outcome more to chance. Their interviewees can at least take consolation knowing that all of the candidates had their interview opportunities unnecessarily restricted. Most interviewers, including those who are well trained and prepared, appreciate an interviewee who volunteers a wealth of information.

The most common problem with interviewers is they talk too much. Like defensive interviewers, they too face the decision process with a restricted pool of information. However, the talkative interviewer is decidedly not defensive. A good interviewee should be able to insert a portion of the interviewee guide. Typically, the talkative interviewer will let the interviewee start to tell a story or make a point and then interrupt with a story or a point of his or her own. The best interviewee strategy is to be a good listener. Listening is probably at the top of this interviewer's job candidate behavior list.

Interviewing the Interviewer

Most employment interviewees fail to ask probing questions of their interviewers. When they do, they usually ask trivial questions about the work environment or benefits. But what an employment interviewee most needs to know about is the job search process. How many people are being interviewed? What are their strengths and weaknesses? When will the decision be made? Who will make it? What are the decision-maker's main concerns? How do the candidates compare so far?

Most job candidates would never think of asking these questions because they assume their interviewers would never answer them. But consider that interviewing is an exercise of power. We use power to cause other people to do things that they might not otherwise have done. What better application of interviewing strategy and tactics than to peek inside the hiring process so you can fine tune your presentation?

We are talking about picking the interviewer's pocket. Two things make this possible. First, most interviewers are unprepared to conduct an interview. Typically they have no guide. They ask questions about skills instead of behavior. When they do ask about behavior, they give away what they are looking for. Their main concern is probably that you will figure out that they are posing. If you don't believe interviewer's are so unprofessional, consider the statistic that most job interviewers make their hiring decision in the first five minutes of the interview—a decision based on how the interviewee is dressed, the firmness of the handshake, and if the experience made them feel good. The second area of vulnerability is inherent in the interview process itself. One of the tacit social rules governing interviews is that it is almost always acceptable to ask a question. This is especially true if the other party has just asked you several questions. It is as if a debt has been accumulated by the interviewer. When the interviewee asks a question in return, the interviewer feels even greater psychological pressure to provide a meaningful answer. There is a rational impetus here as well. How can I expect you to answer my questions if I don't answer yours?

Obviously, interviewing the interviewer requires a degree of finesse. In all rhetorical encounters the ethical appeal is of primary importance. It doesn't matter what an interviewee finds out; if the interviewer has been alienated during the process, the information is useless. The main character traits required of an interviewee are openness and cooperation. Let the interviewer control the interaction well past mid-point in the interview, but don't wait for an invitation. Most employment interviewers ask, "Do you have any questions for me?" as a wrap-up when there is no time left. Start looking for the right segue at about the half-way point. When you are ready to start, don't be subtle. Call attention to what you are doing: "I have a question for you about that . . ." or, "Could I ask you something . . ." The interviewer knows he or she should be asking the questions, but will feel pressure from a more deep-seated social imperative to let the other person take a turn.

The strategy from this point on is to start small and escalate until you have either stripped the interviewer of everything he or she knows, or until the interviewer realizes what is going on and cuts you off. A good first question might ask about the job. If the interviewer asks, "How do you feel about sharing an office?" Answer the question, then, without hesitating, say, "can I ask you a few questions about the office?" If the interviewer responds with, "Let's save your questions for last . . ." then you have been shut down, and you stop. However, in most cases, the interviewer will respond to your question enthusiastically. You find out the new hire will be sharing a computer. Drive the questions deeper, ask, "how did that work for the last person to hold this position?" This is another turning point. If the interviewer answers, the door is open, and you can eventually find out what the previous position-holder's strengths and weaknesses were ("He was a great accountant, but hard to get along with . . ."). Get what you can on this without seeming nosey. The next turning point is to bring the discussion back to the job search: "You can check someone's accounting skills pretty easy, but how can you tell if he or she will fit with your workgroup?" Most interviewers will recognize their selection process is being compromised at this point. They will smile and say something like, "Well, that's why we are doing this interview," and then ask their next question. However, there are some interviewers who are confident enough in their own verbal skills that they will keep sparring with you, and other interviewers who will be happy they get to keep talking and will keep handing out information.

As long as the interviewee is cautious, there is little risk in attempting the interviewer interview. Smart interviewers will respect interviewees who push the envelope and may decide to hire interviewees who do, because they want people with acute rhetorical skills on their team. And naïve interviewers will think the interviewees were good listeners. The key is to push the counter-interview tactic exhaustively, but to stop before it becomes offensive. Keep in mind, every interviewer is different. They have different personalities, different experiences, and different preparation. One interviewer might immediately shut down the line of questioning, another might evaluate the other job candidates and tell the interviewee where he or she ranks.

Lastly, it is necessary to cut the counter-interview off with enough time for the interviewer to ask the job applicant more questions. Finding out about the job search process is only useful if the job applicant can use the information to select and shape answers to forthcoming questions. So, if an interviewee discovered in the counter-interview that the previous employee alienated himself by being aloof, and the interviewer asks, "How do you get along with your coworkers at your present job?" you respond by talking about the office picnic you planned, or the going away party someone is throwing for you.

One of the defining characteristics of rhetoric is the use of enthymeme. The enthymeme is the counterpart of the syllogism. Essentially the difference between syllogism and enthymeme is that the syllogism tells people what to think, and the enthymeme lets them discover things for themselves. It is important that the interviewee make his or her arguments enthymatically. That is, do not say, "I know you are looking for someone who works well under pressure, and I am that person." That is a crude sales pitch; it will be devalued because it is self-serving. Instead, wait for a question about a project you worked on, or a hypothetical scenario, and answer in such a way that the interviewer can experience how you handle pressure through your answer. Additionally, it might be possible to show pleasure in talking about pressure situations. In rhetoric this is called demonstration and signs. The accumulation of demonstrations and signs leaves a stronger impression and lets the interviewer draw a more objective, reliable conclusion.

Unfair Interview Practices

Equal Employment Opportunity laws and regulations do not keep employers from hiring who they choose; they merely try to insure that no one is eliminated from the selection process unfairly and that no one who takes part in the hiring process is treated unfairly. Some EEO violations are clear cut, like never interviewing members of certain racial groups or only accepting job applicants of one gender. Some might be questionable, like an interviewer asking your age or if you are married. Other violations are just silly, like the chain of record stores in Illinois that once had a job application form that asked, "Color of hair, red ___ or other ___."

There is no FBI sting operation to catch and prosecute EEO offenders. These protections are enforced mainly after someone makes a formal complaint or brings suit. If an EEO violation case goes to court, it can be very expensive for the company responsible for the violation. However, potential EEO violations occur in most employment interviews, and the vast majority go unreported. There are several reasons for this. Most of the time, the interviewer and the interviewee are unaware that a violation has occurred. Sometimes the interviewee is aware of a violation, but the violation isn't one that affects eligibility and he or she still wants to be hired, so the violation is overlooked. Other times, the violation occurs, and the applicant has the will and the financial independence to take on the company either by reporting them or by bringing suit.

The United States of America promised freedom to its citizens starting with the Declaration of Independence in 1776, but it has taken a Civil War, the suffrage movement, a decade of civil rights protests, and a complex network of EEO laws and regulations to make that freedom a reality. EEO seems like excessive government intervention to some, and it seems ineffective to others, but it has been the only true battleground for American freedom since the end of World War II.

EEO is effective ultimately because the threat of large fines and settlements generates a cultural sensitivity that is slowly changing hiring and promotion practices. It is not necessary or reasonable that every violation be reported and prosecuted. Job applicants may want to take a practical look at this issue. If you can make a case that hiring or promotion practices are discriminatory and you feel protected or insulated, or you are just willing to take the risk, then report the offenses or hire a lawyer. You may find it financially rewarding, and if not, you have at least weighed in on the battle for fairness and freedom. It is, however, a rare job interview that does not contain some level of EEO violation. A key question to ask is, "Do I want to work for this company?" Sometimes the behavior of an interviewer convinces us that we do not want to work for a company, and sometimes we take a job because we think we can change or ignore what we do not like.

The Salary Question

An interviewer asking a job applicant, "How much do you want to make?" is like a used car salesperson asking a customer, "How much do you want to spend?" The question compromises the trust and goodwill that are necessary for a meaningful interview interaction. The interviewee's answer to the question is irrelevant. Most companies have established salary ranges for jobs, and, if they have not, and they bring in a new accountant one day at $25,000 and another one a week later at $32,000, then they are creating motivation and possible legal problems that could cost them a lot more than the $7,000 they think they saved. The best response to this question is not to answer it.

How do you not answer the salary question? Here are some suggestions. Say that you are interested in the job because it is a good career move or because you want to work for the company and that you will be happy making what other employees with your credentials and responsibilities are making. This is a safe answer, and it subtly explains to the interviewer that the question was inappropriate. If the interviewer does not get the hint and presses for a number, then turn the tables. Ask what the salary range is, or what the person you are replacing made. If an interviewer answers your question, then you can easily answer the interviewer's question. If the interviewer declines, the line of questioning will probably be dropped. If, however, the interviewer persists, then say you have to think about it. Any foray by an interviewer past this point is clear indication of a brutal management culture. Think of how much the company would have to pay you to put up with nonsense like this, add 20 percent to make sure you have no regrets, and quote your number.

One Purdue University Calumet graduate was asked about salary requirements after a series of interviews for a public relations job. He had been asking questions as well as answering them during several days of interviews, and he knew they were already making plans for his future role in their company. He had also discovered what several other people in the company were making. Even though he was just a year out of college and making about $40,000 a year, he estimated that they would pay $65,000, and that is the salary he quoted, even though he would still take the job if it were $45,000. His interviewer smiled, nodded, and said, "I think we can do that."

From the interviewee's perspective, the best time to discuss salary is after you have been offered the job. All of the psychological factors are on the interviewee's side at this point. Typically people making the decision will talk up the favorite candidate to their coworkers. The hiring process is almost completed and the person or committee making the decision wants credit for finding the right candidate. They now need your consent to bring everything to fruition. A dramatic insight to this process was provided in 1999 when the Chicago Bears were hiring the 11th head coach in team history. They called a press conference to announce that they had selected Dave McGinnis and even put his name on the head coach answering machine replacing the name of former coach Dave Wannstedt. But McGinnis had not yet agreed to terms. The Bears postponed the press conference while the owners, Ed McCaskey and his son Michael, pleaded with McGinnis who had decided not to take the job. McGinnis decided he wanted nothing more to do with the McCaskeys, but his salary bargaining power must have been enormous.

Networking

Networking is a misleading term. Everyone has a network. As we work and socialize we get to know people and they get to know us. The impression we make with the people we know transfers to people who only know us by reputation. The notion of creating a network and fabricating a reputation calls to mind people with insincere smiles and hardy handshakes. The best way to network is be hard-working, honest, and productive.

It is true that some professionals never send out resumes after landing their first jobs. All of their other career opportunities came from people they had met and with whom they worked. This is possible because most employers do not know how to probe behavior during a job interview, so every new hire is a tremendous risk. Hiring someone whom they have seen perform, either as a competitor or as a consultant, is their only means of diminishing the role of chance in the hiring process.

This is decidedly not the case for recent college graduates and entry level jobs. The graduate has no professional network, and the company probably has no interaction with people looking for entry level jobs unless they take interns from the university. So, for the college graduate, networking makes sense as a verb. A networking plan that was developed for executives being laid off from the insular Xerox corporation in the late 1970s is a good model. Most graduating seniors should be able to name three people they know in the field they want to enter. Perhaps there is someone you interviewed for a report, someone who spoke to a class and you asked for a business card, and maybe a fellow student who graduated and landed a job already. Send each of these people a resume with a cover letter. Both the cover letter and the resume should be developed around your three key behaviors. The cover letter should be short and say something like "I think when you look at my resume you will see that I am results-oriented, a self-starter, and . . ." The letter could say that you will be calling next week to arrange an appointment to "discuss my opportunities in the profession." Note, you are not asking for a job. If you ask for a job, they will tell you when you call that they do not have a job for you and hang up. But if you ask them to advise you, most professionals feel a responsibility to comply. When you are meeting them, try to implement your interviewee guide, making sure that they understand you are there for advice, not a job. When you are done, ask if they can give you three names of people who might be hiring. Your hosts should be feeling some pressure to help. Psychologically they have just gone through a job interview, but they have no job to offer. Giving you three names lets them off the hook. After the first three advising interviews, you now have nine new names; do the same with them. A month of full time effort should get your resume on the desks and into the files of all the key people in your field; now you just have to wait until one of your contacts has an employee quit or gets overloaded with work and you will get a call.

References

It is possible to hire someone without references just as it is possible to hire someone without a job interview. The reason for the interview and the reference check is the same: to predict how the applicant will perform if he or she is hired. Job applicants in every profession and at every level of management should know what the skills and behavior requirements are for the positions they seek. Both the interview and the references are part of an argument constructed and presented by the applicant to address those requirements.

References are people who vouch for the interviewee's character. There are two types of references. The most effective reference is an informal reference from a mutual acquaintance. This is someone whom the person or people doing the hiring already know. Job search committees generally believe if a reference is obtained from someone with whom they do business or socialize, it is likely to be more objective and the person giving the reference is more accountable for what he or she says. On the other hand, formal references on lists provided by applicants are selected because they hold the applicant in high esteem, and these references are accountable to the applicant, not the person doing the hiring. Thus, references from mutual acquaintances are highly valued, and references provided by the job candidate are not. This is why having a network of business contacts is so useful.

Formal references are still required as part of the hiring routine. Rarely do employers ask for generic letters of reference. Typically they want a list of three names with phone numbers and addresses. Someone from the hiring organization will call the references and conduct a short phone interview. Companies hiring senior management personnel take these reference interviews seriously, but for most jobs, phone reference interviews are so routine and carry so little weight in the hiring process that often the job candidate has been hired before the calls are completed.

The following are recommendations for job applicants who want to make the most out of their references. First, select six reference names, two supervisors, two peers, and two subordinates. If you do not have actual subordinates to pick from, then select people who worked with you on projects where you had a leadership role. Put the six names on one page with headings for the three categories and References at the top. Second, contact the six references and give them copies of your resume and cover letter. Tell them which behaviors you are focusing on. It might help to highlight the sentence in the cover letter that lists them. Third, keep in touch. When you get called for a job interview, that probably means someone is starting to check your references. Call your references and tell them the name of the company and that they should expect to be contacted. Fourth, when you finally accept a job offer, call your references and thank them. Overall, since most employers expect the references to be positive, the relative enthusiasm and cooperativeness of the voice on the phone may be a deciding factor in a close contest.

Fielding Reference Calls

Here are some suggestions if you are serving as a reference for someone else and you want to make a difference. Give the job seeker your home phone number in addition to your business phone number. This makes it more likely the potential employers will find you. When the call comes, try to take it immediately. Remember, it is just a few minutes of your time that may affect someone's entire career. The reference conversation will begin with some standard questions. Some callers will want to verify that you know the person or worked with the person then try to hang up. Don't let them. This is an interview. You have just answered their questions, now they have to answer yours. Try casually asking something about the job. If the interviewer cooperates, try probing a little. See if you can find out about the work environment, the committee making the decision, the last person to hold the job, and, if you really have control of the situation, ask how the search process is going and how your acquaintance compares to the other candidates. As you are listening, identify the company's main concerns and pair them up with one or two anecdotal stories you can relate about the candidate that will address them. Wait until the interviewer is finished and on another subject, then tell your story. "By the way, did Rob tell you about the reunion he organized for our alumni?"

To someone who studies interviewing, it may seem that no one would be gullible enough to go along with this. Yet the potential for using interview skills to influence the outcome of the process is significant. The person providing the reference is an interviewee with needed information and therefore has the most power in the interaction. Even a well trained job interviewer might cautiously participate in the dialogue to see what he or she can learn. But most interviewers are unprepared. Consider the lack of time, the absence of training, and the irrational influences that typify most job interviews. Interviewers in the latter category will tell you everything they know and hang up feeling grateful that you listened to them.

The Cover Letter and Resume

The most common mistake with cover letters and resumes is trying to say too much. No one gets a job from a cover letter. The purpose of the cover letter is to get someone to read your resume. The purpose of the resume is to get invited in for an interview. The purpose of the interview is to get the job. Keep the cover letter short. Three two or three sentence paragraphs should be enough. State why you are writing, mention your three key behaviors, and close. If you are sending the letter to someone on the advice of a mutual acquaintance, say so in the first paragraph, and in the last paragraph state that you will call to see if you can arrange a meeting. You can assume you will get an interview because it is a professional courtesy to the person who told you to make the contact, and saying you will call forces the recipient to read and file the resume.

In most professions, the key to a successful resumé is to be conservative. Use a basic 12 point font like Times Roman, white or light gray or beige paper, and make sure there are no misspellings or grammatical errors. The grammar can be managed by having two or three people with good language skills proofread the resumé. While it is advantageous to get all the feedback you can on grammar and spelling, it is not useful to let people tell you how to lay out the resumé, or what to say or not say. Select a model resumé layout that you know is used in your profession and stay with it.

As a rule, college graduates should have no more than one page. Everyone else should try to keep resumes to two pages. The resume isn't an autobiography, it is just a teaser to make someone curious enough to call you in for an interview. Like all advertising, it will benefit from being brief and easy to read. When trying to decide what to include, consider the job requirements and review your list of three key behaviors.

Under ideal circumstances, the interviewer will note the three behaviors in the cover letter, look for evidence of them in the resume, and unconsciously use them as a guide while conducting the interview.

Chapter Nine

The Survey Interview

Argument by Example

When people fill out survey questionnaires or give shopping or voting preferences to someone over the phone, they become interviewees or *survey respondents*. The interviewers who pass out and collect surveys or call on the phone are part of a larger process where someone else writes the questions, prints them, and trains the people who actually have contact with the interviewees. If those who run this interview process cause a number of survey interviews to be conducted on the same subject using some of the same questions, and if they combine the information gathered from all the interviews, then they will have conducted a survey.

The distinguishing characteristic of the survey interview is that it has no value by itself. The information gathered from a survey interview acquires rhetorical force only after it is added to similar information gathered from other interviews on the same subject and conducted in the same way. Generally speaking, the more people interviewed, the more valuable the data. This is because the survey makes an argument by example. We argue by example when we say that because something happened in the past, it will happen again in the future. This kind of example is called a precedent. The more precedents one has, the more persuasive the argument. A marketing survey composed of 300 interviews with 300 shoppers is more likely to predict sales potential than a marketing survey of 100 interviews of 100 shoppers, and an interview of one shopper has no predictive powers at all.

Qualitative vs. Quantitative Research

There are essentially two categories of interview research. The larger category is called qualitative research. Journalistic and employment interviews are examples of qualitative research. Topics, methods, and applications for qualitative interviews are unlimited. That is because qualitative information has intrinsic value. A witness in a criminal trial is a qualitative interviewee. If the witness is credible, his or her testimony may be enough to influence a decision by a judge or jury. In qualitative research, the content of the interview gives it value regardless of how many people agree or disagree.

The methods and applications of quantitative research are more limited. Many interviews are required, all interviewees must be asked the same questions in the same way, and they must choose from the same answer options. If this is accomplished, then the answers can be tabulated and reported as percentages. If one person thinks handguns should be outlawed, it is insignificant; if 60 percent of registered voters think handguns should be outlawed, then the National Rifle Association has a problem. While the survey process requires many interviews, its methods severely limit what can be researched, and its uses are confined mainly to opinion research for guiding marketing strategies, predicting voter trends, and generalizing about human behavior.

Surveys convert qualitative information into quantitative data by assigning a value or a number to each survey answer. Assigning numbers to answers is called coding. When surveys have been completed, they are collected and the numbers are entered into a tabulation program. It is important that the answer options have the coding numbers printed on the survey so that tabulation can be fast and accurate.

Here is an example of coded telephone survey questions. Note that each question has a number and each answer option has a number. The combination of the question number and the answer number insures that every answer in the survey has a unique code:

4. In the 11th District, seven candidates are running in the 1994 Democratic primary for the U.S. House of Representatives. If the Democratic primary election for the U.S. House of Representatives were being held today, would you vote for . . . {REPEAT CANDIDATES' NAMES AS NEEDED}

William "Bill" Barrett, ... 1
John "Jack" Buchanan, ... 2
Clem Balanoff, ... 3
Frank Giglio, ... 4
Daniel L. Kennedy Jr., ... 5
Dave Neal, or 6
Martin J. "Marty" Gleason? 7
UNCERTAIN 9

5. Now, I'd like you to rate your feelings toward each of the following people as either very favorable, somewhat favorable, somewhat unfavorable, or very unfavorable. If you are not certain, just tell me that. {PROMPT AS NEEDED}

	VERY FAVOR	SOMEWH FAVOR	SOMEWH UNFAVOR	VERY UNFAVOR	DON'T KNOW
A. William "Bill" Barrett	4	3	2	1	9
B. John "Jack" Buchanan	4	3	2	1	9
C. Clem Balanoff	4	3	2	1	9
D. Frank Giglio	4	3	2	1	9
E. George Sangmeister	4	3	2	1	9
F. Daniel L. Kennedy Jr.	4	3	2	1	9
G. Dave Neal	4	3	2	1	9
H. Martin J. "Marty" Gleason	4	3	2	1	9

If an interviewee answers Marty Gleason in the first question, then the answer becomes 4, 7 in the tabulation process. If the answer is Daniel Kennedy, then the answer is entered 4, 5. The second question is more complicated, but still fairly easy and foolproof to tabulate. If someone answers "very favorable" for George Sangmeister, then the answer is entered as 5, E, 4: 5 because it is question five, E because E represents the George Sangmeister line, and 4 because the number four represents the VERY FAVORABLE column.

Public Opinion

Historically, public opinion has had two meanings that are parallel with the two kinds of research. In a qualitative sense, public opinion means public consensus. Consensus is formed when people have open discussion and debate on an issue, and when their objective is to discover the truth or to agree on the best plan. Ideas are stated publicly where they can be challenged and defended. Ideally, after a period of time in open debate, it will be clear that some ideas are better than others. Participants in the debate, if they are being open minded and honest, will arrive at a consensus—that is, they will have tested all the ideas until they can agree on which ones are best, even if those ideas are not the ones they originally supported. This kind of consensus-forming debate is required of juries, but it can take place on a much larger scale. The United States, as a nation, debated issues like independence from England, slavery, the right of workers to organize, and joining the fight against Nazi Germany and reached general consensus on all of them. It has yet to reach consensus about the need to send troops to Vietnam and Iraq or the legal status of abortion. Not all public debate results in consensus, but a faith in the public's ability to form this kind of public opinion is the underlying social principle of democracy.

The purely quantitative face of public opinion is a measure of mere agreement that can take place without being tested in public debate. Agreement without honest and careful discussion can be reached because there is only one viable conclusion and it is apparent to almost everyone, and sometimes it is the result of apathy or emotion or just a hasty decision-making process. This is the public opinion of propaganda, mass hysteria, and tyranny. The framers of the U.S. Constitution wanted to encourage citizens to participate in rational consensus formation and to avoid irrational processes resulting in mere agreement. That is why they created a representative government instead of a true democracy. Congress, for example, is made up of representatives who are elected every two years and senators who are elected every six years. Representatives necessarily must reflect popular sentiment, but senators, being farther removed from the election process, can afford to be more reflective and cautious. The effects of this were clearly seen in 1998 when the House of Representatives voted to impeach President Bill Clinton over a sex scandal and the Senate did not.

The quantitative survey process, because of its methodology, cannot reflect the qualitative process of public consensus formation. Survey public opinion is gathered in private from anonymous interviewees, it is not tested in open debate, and the opinion itself, not the truth or the usefulness of the idea, is the objective of the interview. Thus, survey data do not represent public consensus. In a democratic setting, citing survey results as "public opinion" can be misleading and harmful, even though the research process was performed with great precision.

In the final analysis, public consensus formation is a qualitative social process. It takes place with or without assistance from governments and surveys. Before the Declaration of Independence or the U.S. Constitution was written, public opinion had formed about the need for independence in the 13 colonies. It was formed through conversations in taverns and coffee houses, with the help of public speeches and printed editorials, and in public meeting places. Public opinion formation can be inhibited, but it is not created or eliminated by laws, and it cannot be captured or replaced by survey interviews.

If the distinctions between qualitative and quantitative are not clear, consider this hypothetical situation. You have been accused of a crime you did not commit. During the trial the state has presented extensive circumstantial evidence linking you to a murder—things like the color and make of your car, your general description, and your proximity to the crime. Your attorney has countered by arguing that you had no motive and that you are not a violent person. The prosecution and the defense attorneys have finished and it is time for the jury to decide the case. Which would you prefer, passing out a quick survey where the jury members vote guilty or not guilty with the judge breaking a tie, or dismissing the jury to a sequestered room and not letting them out until they all agree on one verdict?

Uses of Survey Interviews

The value of public opinion surveys, then, is to monitor public consensus, not to replace it. For instance, a survey that explores how much voters know about the current state of the prison system in the United States would be more useful than a survey asking them if they would prefer giving early releases, building more prisons, revamping minimum sentence laws, or leaving things as they are. Even if most people are uninformed, they will still have opinions, and a survey that asks respondents to select from the given options could report that one of them, probably "leaving things as they are," was the most popular. However, an agreement among the uninformed does not constitute a consensus. Knowing there might be a problem, but being uninformed about it, represents only a first stage in the consensus formation process. It is likely that if conditions in the prison system worsen, people will learn more from news and entertainment media, conversations with friends, and from personal experience. If public discussion begins in earnest, it may proceed until everyone is working with roughly the same pool of information. Next, people will speculate about solutions to the problem, and that speculation will be challenged. Eventually some or one of the speculative options might acquire the force of consensus, and that consensus will influence the actions of the state. Opinion polling is best used to map what people know and attempt to gauge the progress of the consensus formation process.

About the only time a survey can be used to reveal actual public consensus is after consensus has formed, and then there would be little need for the survey except as a confirmation or measurement tool for news agencies or public relations strategists. There are two exceptions to this, however, and they are large ones. One is when the public in question has not and probably will not reach a consensus. Public discussion takes place in a finite universe where competing issues vie for attention on the public consciousness. If the prison system problem never reaches a crisis state, chances are that it will never attract enough public attention to ignite debate. In this case, an aggregate of private opinions—a survey report on the popularity of various options—provides the most useful information available. The other exception is when two relatively equal consensus formations have occurred. This was the case with the slavery issue just prior to the Civil War, and it is the case now with abortion. Here the consensus process has resulted in two competing conclusions. A survey asking interviewees if abortion should be legal or illegal could produce an accurate account of the outcome of two independent consensus formation processes.

All public issues fall into these three categories: consensus formation, non-consensus formation, and dual or multiple consensus formation. This is a broad, pragmatic system for categorizing public issues for research purposes. It should be noted that history eventually moves everything into the first category. That is, given enough time, perspective will probably provide the consensus that was unattainable through public debate.

Survey Methodology

Knowledge of private opinions, then while it does not have the finality and force of public consensus, can still be of value. If surveys are conducted to strict research standards, they can be highly accurate in producing what is best described as an aggregate of private opinions.

Survey methodology is a body of knowledge that prescribes standards and guidelines for producing useful survey data. Developing survey methodology is an ongoing process that has benefited from over 100 years of testing and refinement. The methodology requires that before conducting a survey one identify a target public called a *population* by survey researchers, select a sample, write and test the survey, and train survey interviewers. The methodology also addresses ways of tabulating the survey data.

Target Public

For survey researchers and public relations practitioners there is no public. Instead they see a landscape of publics. Almost all political surveys attempt to limit their pool of interviewees to registered voters who are likely to vote. And marketing surveys want only to interview people who are eligible to purchase their products. A sixteen year old who answers a phone call from a survey interviewer will not be allowed to participate in the political interview, but might have been highly eligible for a marketing survey interview for Trek bicycles or Play Station III. Some publics constitute themselves, like the American Association of Retired People, other publics are abstractions, like Baby Boomers and Gen-Xers. The first task in putting together a survey project is to decide how to configure the public from whom the interviewees will be selected.

The best way to identify the target public is to start with the end in mind. Consider how the information will be used. Perhaps a mayoral candidate has strong opinions on several issues and needs to know which ones will help the campaign and which ones will hurt the campaign. The campaign staff needs to identify and survey only those people who are likely to vote in the mayoral election. Analysis turns up a small group. Only about half of those eligible to vote are registered to vote. Only half of the registered voters ever cast a vote. And, according to our hypothetical analysis, only 20 percent of people who cast votes in general elections bother to vote in local elections. By randomly interviewing only members of this select group, speeches, handouts, and advertising can all be directed at issues most likely to get the attention and win the approval of the select few who will decide the election.

Targeting publics can go even further. If a survey asks the right questions, the respondents can be subdivided into even more specialized groups. Chances are that someone who bothers to vote in off-year local elections not only knows more about local issues, but also has strong allegiances to certain candidates and community leaders. Sometimes election campaign surveys not only ask about issues but also about other office-holders. Then they ask interviewees which neighborhoods they live in. Armed with this information a campaign staff can print different campaign handouts for different neighborhoods, each listing the issues and quoting the endorsements identified as most salient and popular with those voters in those neighborhoods.

Census

Once a target public has been selected, interviews can be conducted to reveal what members of that public think about the research topic. The best way to discover what a group of people think is usually to conduct interviews with the entire group. This is called a census, not a survey. A survey collects data from a sample. Just like the U.S. census, a census attempts to reach everyone in the target public. If the target public is small enough, and if the research team has the resources, then a census is the preferable method for gathering quantitative interview data. Typically employee attitude research is conducted as a census because the company has the access and the resources to reach every member of its target group. When a census is completed, it reveals what everyone in the group believed about its topic at the time it was taken.

The biggest challenges when conducting a census are locating everyone in the target public, getting full cooperation, and completing the survey in a short time frame. Imagine how difficult it would be to conduct a census survey of students at a university. Students attend classes at different times, and on any given day some who are supposed to be in attendance are home sick, stuck in traffic, or just playing hooky. Other students have moved home for a semester to work on their dissertations, or are taking classes on-line, or have just dropped out. Deciding who is eligible to participate and getting completed survey interviews from them are two halves of a formula that can require a good deal of analysis and a good deal more legwork.

Every census report should devote a part of its methodology section to explaining why and how the target public was constituted and who should have been included but was not. It is also appropriate for the census team to detail the extent to which they tried to acquire the missing interviews. The rhetorical power of a census is that it doesn't attempt to predict anything. As opposed to a report claiming that 300 employee interviews are an example of what the entire population of 5,000 employees thinks, the census is a statement of fact. However, to speak with this authority, the census report has to include either every member of the group or make it clear that it at least includes every accessible member of the group.

Random Sample Surveys

The random sample survey is a fast, less expensive way of predicting the results of a census without actually conducting a census. Essentially, the random sample survey uses rhetorical arguments of example and probability as a substitute for hard evidence. It is statistically proven that a random sample, if it is large enough, can produce the same results as a census within three percentage points plus or minus. Random selection is more important than the size of the sample. If a target population has 10,000 members and 400 are randomly selected and surveyed, that result will be more accurate than conducting the same survey with 800 interviewees who were not randomly selected.

Using examples to predict something is not just a rhetorical strategy: it is a necessary cognitive process. All of us use examples to navigate through our physical and social environments. Cars that slide off the road during the year's first snowstorm are examples that cause other drivers to slow down. Furthermore, we know that others are using examples to interpret the world, and we know that by creating examples we may be able to influence their perceptions.

The difference between random and non-random examples is the degree of predictability. If three members of a neighborhood speak against plans to build a Wal-Mart, then the city council members might see them as examples of all of the members of that neighborhood and conclude that there would be trouble if they granted Wal-Mart a building permit. To help support this impression one member of the neighborhood might say, "I am a mother, and I am concerned about the increase in traffic and the safety of my children." Another neighborhood member might claim, "I bought my house as an investment, and my property value will decrease if I am next door to a busy parking lot." The third member of the neighborhood might say she owns a small shop and is afraid she will lose business. They could be the only three people in a neighborhood of 3,000 who oppose the proposed Wal-Mart, but they present themselves as examples of larger groups to give weight to their arguments.

Random sample surveys, if they are performed well, can take a cognitive process that is basically guesswork and turn it into a highly probable prediction. The example of the three citizens at the city council meeting is self-selection. These people choose to attend the meeting and give their opinions. A wise councilmember would not let this influence his or her decision. Holding an open meeting in the neighborhood and listening to the discussion is a better way to determine if there is a consensus. If that is not possible, or if meetings have already taken place, then a random sample survey is the best way to read public opinion in the target group.

Random samples are drawn by chance from a pool of potential respondents that includes everyone from the target public and no one else. Ideally, everyone in the target public must have an equal chance of being drawn. As a rule of thumb, 400 randomly selected interviewees can be used to predict the census of any size group. This number is determined more by the mathematical requirements of randomness than by the size of the group. That means that if the target public is 4,000 or 4,000,000, a random sample of 400 may suffice.

Reliability, Replicability, and Validity

The survey interview process attempts to ask objective questions in a uniform way so the answers can be counted and represented as percentages. However, converting human communication into logical symbols is an impossible task. Mathematics is a language of pure logic, and rhetoric is that which cannot be quantified. Quantifying answers to questions about opinions and human experience is, in classical terms, turning enthymemes into syllogisms. If this were possible, there would be no need for the rhetorical arts. If anticipating and providing for future actions and understanding human nature could be accomplished mathematically, algorithms would replace public debates, two party elections, and theories of human behavior. Absurd as this might sound, it was actually one side of a great debate in the history of the philosophy of science, and the public's faith and reliance on survey data today is part of its legacy. A balanced approach to survey methodology holds scientific standards like reliability, replicability, and validity as goals, not absolute standards.

Reliability refers to the accuracy of a measurement. In survey research, a survey question and its answers are measurements. To manage reliability, a survey question writer tests a survey question on members of the target public and adjusts the wording to make it as simple, clear, and precise as possible. An inherent problem is that no two people will have identical interpretations of a question, so the survey writer settles for question wording that is as clear and precise as possible, given the constraints and conflicts imposed by particular human subjects and the printed word. For example, a survey question that asks, "How long does it take you to get to work?" is relatively unreliable. Some interviewees might pick their fastest day, some their slowest. Some might count time from when they get up from bed until when they sit down at their desks, and others might count only time spent in their cars. Even respondents who had similar understandings of the question could have answers that vary from "50 minutes" to "just under an hour." The question is made more reliable if it is rewritten to ask: "In minutes, how long did it take you to drive to work today?" This version of the question is more reliable because it is more precise, containing beginning and ending markers and imposing a common measurement—minutes. As much as it is possible, the question wording should cause all interviewees to have the same understanding and attempt to provide the same kind of information. If 400 survey interview respondents answer this question in a period of a week, the number of minutes can be added and divided by 400, and it will provide a reasonably accurate measure of the average amount of time it takes someone to drive from a house in Rockford, Illinois, to an office in downtown Chicago.

Replicability is a theoretical test. The replicability test asks, could someone use the same survey, and the same methods, under the same conditions and come up with the same results. This test is basically a character proof for the survey process. While the results of the survey will always be open to interpretation, a replicability test at least insures that the research process itself met certain objective standards.

Unlike reliability and replicability which address the survey interview itself, validity is concerned with the correctness of what is being measured—in other words, are you measuring what you purport to measure? If a survey written in Great Britain that asked, "Have you been to surgery in the last year?" were used in Philadelphia, it would be consistently misunderstood. In America surgery refers to procedures done in an operating room; in Great Britain it means a doctor's office. Because all survey respondents in Philadelphia would misinterpret the question in the same way, one could say that the survey is reliable and replicable. Yet, the survey would be useless; it would not be valid.

Survey Effects

A myriad of problems and paradoxes surround the survey research paradigm, not the least of which is the effect the survey itself has on the formation of public consensus. A survey researcher, for instance, can introduce an issue into public debate by making it the subject of a survey. The apparent swell of popular support for laws against desecrating the American Flag was probably the result of self-perpetuating surveys and news stories about a topic that otherwise would have had little currency in public discourse. Also, once the results of the survey have been reported, there is the possibility that many who would have engaged in debate will decline because the survey results created the appearance of a public consensus. Concerns that reporting exit polls from the East Coast causes lower voter turnout in California are based on this assumption. Ironically, qualitative information cannot be quantified, yet quantitative data can be qualified. That is why a survey, which may have measured nothing, can still influence the outcome of a qualitative public debate.

Pseudo-surveys and Common Methodological Problems

Most of the complexities and uncertainties of survey research discussed so far are unavoidable even in the most rigorous professional research environments. But many surveys, perhaps the majority, are conducted outside of the professional framework. Their problems and the problems they create are significantly greater. Before the enforcement of calling restrictions, the most common form of survey was a ruse that either attempted to transition the survey call into a sales call or collected data to be used later for future targeted marketing calls and mailings. Actual survey calls are quite rare, and these pseudo-survey marketing calls became the most typical phone interview experience for most Americans. The result is a public that is suspicious and highly resistant to phone survey interviews.

Political campaigns often conduct well-run, professional survey projects to track public opinion on important campaign issues. However, they also frequently use tactics similar to an unethical bait and switch sales tactic. The caller will claim to be conducting an election poll and ask who you are voting for. The survey is really more like a census of names and phone numbers taken from voter lists. Interviewees who say they are voting for the candidate sponsoring the survey are put on a priority list, and anyone who is unsure or who is voting for the opposition will be discarded. Starting approximately a week before the election, the priority voters will get up to three callbacks reminding them to vote. On election day, the campaign may have someone at the polling place checking off the priority voters as they pass through. Anyone who has not voted by noon will be given another call and offered a ride. All this is done without the campaign staff ever having to identify themselves with a particular candidate or political party.

The most reprehensible use of survey research is to write, conduct, and report the survey in a way that deliberately creates a false impression. Political candidates know that whoever is perceived as the most likely to win the election will probably receive the most money from campaign contributions. This is because some companies want the candidate to be beholden to them. They will even donate money to more than one candidate in a race just to make sure they backed the winner. The candidate who first leads in the election polling has the best chance of collecting donations, and the donations increase that candidate's chances of winning. Some pseudo-survey houses take advantage of this phenomena and offer surveys that skew the results to make their clients appear to be leading their races.

Another common problem with survey projects is they may be conducted by people who do not understand how to select random samples, ask relatively objective questions, or tabulate the data using appropriate statistical procedures. A poorly run survey project can be worse than no survey at all, as it is better not to know public opinion than to operate under false assumptions. One should always ask questions like who conducted this survey, what was the size of the sample, how were they selected? In this sense, survey research is like the practice of medicine. Anyone can recommend a cure, but the professional credentials and methods of board certified physicians distinguish the informed medical assessment from potentially dangerous alternatives.

The individual's opinion is evasive, the group's a vapor. Public opinion does not lend itself to scientific research the way biology or astronomy do. A professional survey researcher will claim only that the data-gathering procedure is as objective as possible and that the results are statistically accurate at the moment the survey is completed. Yet well-researched survey data usually represent the best information available to help understand and even predict public consensus. Public opinion may be a reification, but we constantly research it, improve our methods, and study the results. In the final analysis the practical application of survey data justifies its precarious epistomology. Individual opinions are drops of water in an ocean and public opinion its currents and eddies. On the one hand you cannot predict how throwing a rock into the water will displace the fluid molecules, but on the other hand, you know a ripple when you see one.

Chapter 10

Writing the Survey

Arrangement

Most public opinion and marketing surveys are divided into five parts: introduction, screening questions, topic questions, demographics, and closing. Interviewees need to know about the survey and the people conducting it before they will consent to be interviewed; this information necessarily comes first in the survey. Next, the survey interviewer must be sure that the interviewee is a member of the target public. This is accomplished by asking screening questions. A marketing survey for an automaker might ask if the respondent has a drivers' license. If the answer is no, the survey is terminated. Once the introduction and filter questions are accomplished, the body of the survey can ask the important questions related to the survey's purpose. Lastly, to help with analysis, the survey asks questions about the interviewee. These are called demographics questions. Age, race, education, income, and location of residence are common subjects of demographic questions. The demographics questions come last because they are personal, and it is more likely that the interviewee will answer them after becoming somewhat acquainted with the interviewer. Also, placing them at the end of the questionnaire decreases the chance that respondents will hang up before rapport is built up. Finally, the survey has a brief but polite closing section. Usually this is just a sentence saying that the survey is complete and thanking the interviewee.

Another consideration under arrangement is contingency questions. Contingency questions are for target publics within the target public. A research survey on marriage might include several questions about children. It would be a waste of time to have all interviewees answer questions about children since not all married couples have children. To streamline the survey, all the general questions about marriage could be placed first after the introduction and the screener questions. All the questions about children could be placed after the general marriage questions and before the demographics section. The first question in the children section could ask: "Do you have children?" If the answer is yes, then the interviewee would continue. If the answer is no, then the interviewee would be asked to skip the children section and go straight to the final section on demographics.

Types of Surveys

All surveys must be typed and printed. This is the first rule in making them reliable and replicable. If different interviewees hear or read the questions differently, then their responses will not be comparable and cannot be converted into quantitative data. The wording and layout of surveys depends on how the interview will be administered. Some surveys are to be read and filled out by the interviewee. Some are to be read to the interviewee in person, and some to be read to the interviewee over the phone. The main difference in the three types of surveys is that those that require an interviewer to read the questions to the interviewee also contain instructions to be read by the interviewer only. These interviewer instructions are in all upper case letters. An example from the marriage survey interview might read: How many years have you been married? ___0 to 5, ___5 to 10, ___11 to 15, ___16 to 25, or ___26 or more [REPEAT ANSWER OPTIONS IF NECESSARY]. The interviewer knows to read the question out loud because it is printed in upper and lower case letters. That part that says "[REPEAT ANSWER OPTIONS IF NECESSARY]" does not get read out loud because it is in all upper case letters.

Introduction

The introduction should include the topic and the purpose of the survey, the name of the interviewer, the survey sponsor, and an orientation. Lastly, it should ask the interviewee for permission to continue. All of this needs to be accomplished quickly because of all the forms of interviews; the survey interview is the one where the interviewee is often least motivated to participate. Depending on how it is worded, the introduction can either motivate the interviewee to participate, or give the interviewee an excuse to not participate.

Survey introductions are essentially short speeches or essays presented to persuade someone else to speak. Since classical times, the introduction's most important strategic objective has been to make a character appeal. The character appeal basically argues that the audience should listen to the speaker because he or she is honest and knowledgeable and has goodwill. Honesty and goodwill are most important for a survey introduction, especially after the public has been put off by years of marketing and sales representatives using pseudo-surveys to take advantage of potential survey respondents. Simply saying that you are honest and have goodwill is not effective, however. In fact, it will make most people suspicious. Honesty and goodwill have to be demonstrated. In the case of the survey introduction they are demonstrated by stating the interviewer's name, the topic and purpose of the survey, and the sponsor, and by providing an orientation. Since pseudo-surveys convey little if any of this information, an added benefit of being forthcoming is that it helps distinguish the legitimate survey from its imitators.

Here is an introduction from an actual political survey. Read it and consider if it meets the above requirements:

> My name is _____, and I'm calling from Thomas Roach and Associates Research. We're conducting a short survey of 11th district residents concerning local issues. The survey will only take about five minutes and I would really appreciate your help.
>
> May I please speak with someone in your household who is registered to vote? {REPEAT INTRO IF ANOTHER PERSON COMES TO PHONE}

Note that this introduction states both the name of the interviewer and the name of the organization conducting the survey. The survey was paid for by the Marty Gleason for U.S. Congress Campaign Committee, but that is not included because it would bias the survey if the interviewees knew which candidate had commissioned it. The topic and purpose are general but not concealed—11th district residents are being asked about "local issues." The orientation requirement is fulfilled by stating the topic and noting that it will take "about five minutes" to complete the survey. Goodwill is suggested by the words "I would really appreciate your help," and "May I please speak . . ." The interviewer, instead of trying to be pushy or persuasive, acknowledges that it is the interviewee who is doing the interviewer the favor. The word "please" in the last sentence finally makes the appeal for assistance after all the information is out. This is followed by the line in all upper case letters, "REPEAT INTRO IF . . ." which is not read out loud. It reminds the interviewer that all interviewees need to hear the introduction and it should be repeated if someone else is directed to the phone. Also of note is the brevity of this introduction. Honesty and goodwill are hinted at by the language of the introduction, but some of the character of the interviewers and their organization is implied by the efficient way they introduce themselves and their project. This may seem trivial, but consider how much less likely interviewees might be to cooperate if the introduction had been unclear, wordy, or redundant. Rhetoricians have always taught that the best argument for character is made by the quality of the speech itself. Thus, the quality of the introduction foretells the quality of the survey interview that follows it.

The official 1990 U.S. Census Form told reader interviewees that they were required by law to participate, but it still offered a persuasive good-will character proof. Its first paragraph read: "Thank you for taking time to complete and return this census questionnaire. It's important to you, your community, and the Nation."

Screener Questions

Screener questions are usually necessary in surveys and censuses. Voter surveys usually ask for a registered voter in the introduction and then ask at least two filter questions after that. Here are the filter questions from the Marty Gleason for Congress survey:

1. First, I need to confirm that you are currently registered to vote in Will Co.

    YES 1
    NO 2   {POLITELY TERMINATE}
    DON'T KNOW 9   {POLITELY TERMINATE}

2. How likely is it that you will vote in the upcoming November 2004 general election? Is it . . . .

    very likely, ... 4
    somewhat likely, ... 3
    somewhat unlikely, or 2   {POLITELY TERMINATE}
    very unlikely? 1   {POLITELY TERMINATE}
    UNCERTAIN 9   {POLITELY TERMINATE}

Anyone who is not registered to vote or admits that it is unlikely that he or she will vote is eliminated from the survey. Political campaigns have to eliminate non-voters so that the survey results will match the election results. Also, note the use of upper and lower case letters in the phone survey. Question one is read to the interviewee, but not its answer options. For question two the answer options are lower case and are read with the question.

Marketing surveys usually choose potential customers as their target groups. If a marketing survey is being conducted for a breakfast cereal, the target public is the person who buys the cereal, not necessarily the person who wants to eat the cereal. The key filter question for this type of survey might ask the respondent if he or she is the one who usually does the grocery shopping.

The Body of the Survey

Survey questions normally are all closed and written in advance, so there is no opportunity for the interviewer to probe. However, almost every other aspect of the qualitative interview has a counterpart in the body of the survey interview. The body is the part of the survey where the interviewee is asked questions about the survey subject. This is generally organized the way a qualitative interview should be organized. The interview is a walk through interior space that the interviewer and interviewee take together. It should be structured to facilitate understanding and recollection. This means grouping subtopics together and starting each topic with the easiest to remember and easiest to answer questions and working toward the more difficult ones. Any question used in a qualitative interview can be used in a survey, provided they can be converted from open to closed.

Probing with Contingency Questions

Sometimes it is possible to write a planned probing sequence into a survey. Here is an example from a student survey on road construction in Northwest Indiana:

8. During the month of September, was traffic ever backed up in this construction area when you drove through it, or not?

     YES. 1
     NO. 2   {SKIP TO QUESTION 10}
     DON'T KNOW. 9   {SKIP TO QUESTION 10}

9. Think about the last time traffic was backed up for five minutes or more. Approximately how long was the delay in this area?

     5-10 minutes 1
     11-15 minutes 2
     16-20 minutes 3
     20-30 minutes 4
     more than 30 minutes . . . 5
     UNCERTAIN 9

10. How would you rate the State of Indiana for the way they handled this construction project? Would you say . . .

excellent 1
good. 2
fair. 3
poor 4
UNCERTAIN 9

If the interviewee experienced no delays, then there is no point wasting time asking about the length of the delay in question 9, so the interviewer instructions in this phone survey tell the interviewer in all upper case letters to take the interviewee directly to question 10. However, if the interviewee experienced a delay, then questions 8, 9, and 10 function as a crude probing sequence where we learn about the interviewee being delayed and how long the delay lasted and then get an evaluation of the state's performance.

To anyone who understands the power of spontaneous probing, planned probing is an oxymoron. Yet, if one has prepared for the survey by conducting qualitative interviews with the target public, and if several interviewees had similar response patterns on certain topics, then it is not unreasonable to write a probing sequence into the survey in the form of filter questions. For instance, if a marketing survey on restaurants asks: "On the average, do you make purchases at fast food restaurants at least once a week, or not?" the interview instructions could either send the interviewee to another fast food question if the answer is yes or to the next section of the survey if the answer is no. The next question in the yes sequence might be: "Which fast food restaurant did you go to most recently?" Answer options would include all the national chains and "other." If an interviewee selects Burger King, and qualitative research has indicated that some people prefer Burger King for its open-flame cooking method, then the next contingency question might ask: "Why did you choose Burger King? Is it . . ." and one of the answer options could include "Burger King is the closest fast food restaurant to where I live or work," and "I prefer open-flame cooking." If the interviewee selects the answer "Burger King is closest . . .", then the interviewee would be directed to skip to the next sections. If "I prefer open . . ." is selected, then the interviewee could be directed to the next contingency question: "Why do you prefer open-flame cooking?" If qualitative interviews turned up two main reasons, then they would be represented as answer options: "Because it tastes better" and "I think it is healthier." Guided by pre-survey qualitative research, an interview section could continue like this indefinitely as long as the data might be useful.

Open-ended Survey Questions

Open-ended questions represent qualitative not quantitative research. Surveys can ask open questions but it is extremely difficult to process qualitative answers with the rest of the quantitative data. The most efficient use of the open answer option is at the end of a series of other answer options. A demographic question might ask where the interviewee was born. The answer options would include "United States," "Mexico," and "Canada," but it would be impractical to list every nation in the world. After providing a list of perhaps two dozen most likely countries, the last option could be "other" followed by a line where the name of the nation of birth could be written in. In a sense, the question is really closed, since there are a finite number of answer options. Each country of birth that comes up can be assigned a number to be processed with the rest of the quantitative data. "What year were you born?" is an example that requires no conversion since the answer is already a number.

The difficulty of incorporating open questions comes when the answers require interpretation on the part of the interviewer or the person tabulating the results. If a survey on national politics includes the question "What do you think will be the most lasting impact of President George W. Bush's administration?" the list of potential answers is incalculable. For tabulation purposes the answers must be sorted into a matrix of categories involving the economy, the wars in Iraq and Afghanistan, response to 9/11, etc. Many responses would match up, but some would not, and some might defy interpretation. Usually, when surveys ask open-ended questions that do not fall into predictable patterns, they refrain from reporting the responses in the same statistical context as the quantitative data. That is, instead of giving percentages, they limit the assessment to something more general like "The most frequent response referenced Iraq with 22 percent . . ." Typically, if a project includes open questions, then the survey report at least has an addendum with a list of all the responses. Even when the data are difficult to quantify, reading the qualitative responses can provide an intuitive glimpse of public opinion that goes beyond the limitations of the tabulated results.

Specific Questions for Specific Answers

Surveys are most efficient when they ask people for concrete information. There is always room for error, but less can go wrong when the question asks for observable, finite data like "What is the last year in school that you completed?" or "Do you personally own a gun, or not?" If the selected answer to the education question is "Twelfth Grade" then, assuming the interviewee understood the question and remembered correctly, he or she finished high school and either did not attend college or attended but did not complete one year of studies. To the extent that it can be done, it is desirable to phrase survey questions and answer options so they are as concrete as possible. For instance "How educated are you? ___Very Educated, ___Somewhat Educated, or ___Uneducated" is less useful than the version that asks for the last year of school that was completed. Very, somewhat, and uneducated are vague descriptions by comparison. Some people might think a high school diploma qualifies for very educated, and others might think very educated implies a Ph.D. For the same reason, a survey does not ask are you young, middle aged or old, when it can ask "In what year were you born?" Essentially, the more vague a question is, the more the answer represents opinion and the less it represents reportable facts. Someone might be 55 years old but feel young. Asking a telephone survey interviewee, are you young, is more likely to field a broad qualitative opinion, and asking what year were you born in is more likely to field factual data.

Specific questions are useful even when the objective of the survey is to produce a broad qualitative assessment of a situation or experience. For example, a survey on the amount of homework assigned at a particular university could simply ask respondents, "How much homework would you say students are expected to perform at your university in one week? ___ less than 10 hours, ___ 11 to 20 hours, ___ 21 to 30 hours, or ___ 31 hours or more?" Can you write a more specific question to measure teaching quality? Consider this: "How much homework would you say you performed last week? ___ less than 10 hours, ___ 11 to 20 hours, ___ 21 to 30 hours, or ___ 31 hours or more?" The first question asks the interviewee to remember every class he or she took and consider all the anecdotal information gathered from other students and come up with an average amount of homework for everyone at the university. The second question asks each respondent about his or her experience the previous week. When all the interviews using the more specific question are completed, the responses will be averaged to arrive at a measure of time spent doing homework that, while it is still subjective, is based more on observable data and less on opinion and guesswork.

Can the question be even more specific? Yes, it can ask the interviewee how much homework he or she did the previous day. This eliminates the need for the interviewee to average seven days of homework. One might think questions that are this specific are potentially misleading because a particular student might have had no homework, or have been sick and unable to do homework the previous day. While this might be a problem in a single qualitative interview, it is not a problem for a quantitative interview. If the quantitative interview is one of many random interviews which will be averaged together, the student who did no homework will be balanced by another student who studied for two exams and wrote a research paper on the previous day. Thus, while an interviewee's report of doing no homework may be atypical, as one of 400 or more random interviews it participates in the creation of an accurate picture of the amount of homework at the university as a whole.

Opinion Questions on Surveys

Sometimes discovering opinion is as important, or more important, than discovering observable facts. In this case it is desirable to force the interviewee to make a broad assessment of an issue or topic. The above example assessed the average number of hours spent doing homework. But if the survey also intended to measure student opinion of the amount of homework required at the university, then it would need to ask the question in a way that forces a student interviewee to answer with an opinion not an observation. Literally, the question might be "Overall, how do you feel about the amount of homework . . .?"

Here is an example of a survey that does both. In an employee attitude survey one question might attempt to assess the relationship between hourly employees and supervisors. This could be measured in part by asking the employees for concrete indicators of supervisor behavior. In this case the more specific the question the better. These questions might include: "When did you last receive a formal performance appraisal from your supervisor?" and "Think of the last meeting you attended with your supervisor. Who talked more at the meeting? Was it ___ you, ___ your supervisor, ___ or did you each talk about half of the time? These questions meet the requirement of collecting relatively observable data and leave the overall assessment to the survey process as a whole. However, it is also useful for an employee attitude survey to measure overall employee opinions about supervisors. The focus of this measurement is not the supervisor, but the employee, and not just the employee's experience, but the employee's opinion. The employee opinion question might be: "On a scale of one to ten with ten being high and one being low, how would you rate your boss as a mentor?" Armed with data from these two types of questions, survey analysis might be able to point out that supervisors with low mentor ratings were the ones who were least likely to provide effective formal employee evaluation.

Likert-scale

Some survey questions like Likert-scale attempt to go beyond getting a quick response. They ask the interviewees to consider something and provide the answer that comes closest to representing how they feel about it. Typically these questions are used to gauge not just opinion, but opinion strength. Likert-scale questions are really statements. Usually they state an opinion. Then they ask the interviewee how strongly he or she agreed or disagreed with the opinion statement. There are at least two advantages to this kind of question strategy. First, because it overtly states an opinion the question is more likely to provoke a thoughtful response. Second, the answer options measure not just if the interviewee agreed or disagreed, but how strongly the interviewee agreed or disagreed.

Here is a Likert-scale question with five answer options from a telephone survey:

> Next I am going to read a statement. Please tell me if you strongly agree, agree, have no opinion, disagree, or strongly disagree with the statement:
>
> I am financially better off today than I was four years ago. Do you strongly agree, agree, have no opinion, disagree, or strongly disagree? [REPEAT IF NECESSARY]
>
> ___ STRONGLY AGREE
> ___ AGREE
> ___ NO OPINION
> ___ DISAGREE
> ___ STRONGLY DISAGREE

The question above has a "no opinion" option, but often surveys leave out this middle option and force interviewees to decide how they feel. Repeated use of questions like this has shown that as many as one third or more of interviewees will take the neutral response option if it is available. This may be because it requires less effort, or because the interviewee has not given the issue much thought. In most cases it is desirable to leave out the neutral option and force the interviewee to choose. On a phone survey, if the neutral option is omitted, it can still appear as an unread answer option for the interviewer to check if the interviewee is unable to answer.

Ranking

Another way to get thoughtful answers from survey respondents is to ask them to stack rank answer options. This is most easily done in self-administered questionnaires. Interviewees are asked to study a list of answer options. Instead of picking the one that best answers the question, they rank all of the answers from the one that best fits down to the one that least fits the assessment requirement. Usually the answers are presented in a column with a blank line in front of each where the interviewee can place a number. A typical ranking, or ordinal scale, will give the interviewee five answers to number:

> Following is a list of five types of urban crimes. Please write a number between 1 and 5 next to each item. Put 1 next to the crime that you are most concerned about. Put 5 next to the crime you are least concerned about. Please use each number only once.
>
> ___ Drug use and drug trafficking
> ___ Home invasion
> ___ Consumer fraud
> ___ Gang violence
> ___ Auto theft

A self-administered survey can list more than five items, but a phone survey should not list more than three, as it is difficult for most people to entertain more than three items if they cannot see them.

Demographics

Demographics questions usually are not the subject of the survey. They collect data about the interviewees that help survey analysts understand the answers to the questions relating to the topic of the survey. Typically they ask for age, race, income, education, etc. A candidate in a county election might conduct a survey mainly to find out if voters recognize his or her name, and for whom they are intending to vote. These questions would be in the body of the survey. If the survey results indicate that only 50 percent of the voters recognize the candidate's name, then it would be useful to spend more time campaigning in the areas where the candidate is relatively less known. This can be learned if the survey asked interviewees to select the city where they live. If the survey were for a Porter County Indiana Sheriff's race, then the questions would be something like "Which city or town do you live in or live closest to in Porter County?" Once the survey data have been entered on a computer using standard survey processing software like SPSS, the answers to the name recognition questions can be analyzed in conjunction with the answers to the "city or town" question. Typically this is displayed as a chart called a crosstab. It may turn out that the candidate is well known in rural areas, but has virtually no name recognition in the city of Portage. Since Portage represents a significant block of voters in Porter County, the campaign can turn its focus and resources to Portage. In a close election, this information could be the difference between winning and losing the race. Note, however, that it would do the campaign little good to discover the candidates low name recognition if it did not also know where to find the voters who it needed to reach with advertising and campaign appearances.

Nominal Scales

The most common questions in the demographics section are nominal and ordinal scale questions. An nominal scale question provides mutually exclusive variables and asks the interviewee to choose one. A question asking if the respondent is male or female is nominal. An ordinal scale is like a nominal scale except the answer options are ordered. Questions about income and level of education are almost always nominal scale questions:

Which best describes the level of education you have completed?

___ Ph.D.
___ Masters degree
___ Bachelors degree
___ Community College two-year degree
___ High School diploma
___ One or more years of high school
___ Less than one year of high school

Note that the answer options have to be exhaustive. The "Less than one year of high school" answer option covers everyone with less than one year, including those who have no formal education at all. It is also important that the answer options do not overlap. An ordinal scale question about income might have answer options like this:

Select the figure that best represents your yearly income rounded off to the nearest thousand dollars.

___ $100,000 or more
___ $50,000 to $99,999
___ $25,000 to $49,999
___ Less than $25,000

Closing

Surveys are self-consciously polite. By being civil, the interviewer creates an atmosphere where the interviewee feels compelled to be civil as well. This should be carried through to the very end of the survey where only two things are necessary. One, tell the interviewee that you are finished, and two, thank the interviewee for cooperating. Here is a good basic conclusion for a telephone survey: "Thank you very much for your time; that completes the survey."

Sometimes the survey is part of an ongoing or larger research project, and it may be desirable to ask the interviewee if he or she would be willing to participate in further research. Here is a sample from a telephone survey:

> Finally, as part of our continuing research, we may want to call some people back and ask a few more questions. Would that be o.k.?
>
> YES   1
>
> {IF YES} Could I please have your first name, so if we call back we will know who to ask for? _____
>
> NO   2

Gender Question

Gender is a necessary demographics question in almost all survey research. It can be a straight-forward question in self-administered surveys, but becomes problematic in telephone surveys. By most standards it is impolite to ask people if they are male or female. For this reason telephone surveys sometimes put the gender questions in upper case letters at the end of the survey.

> GENDER: MALE   1   FEMALE   2

After thanking the interviewee and hanging up, the interviewer reads the last question and makes a best guess.

Supplemental Materials

(The following material has been condensed.)

Thomas Roach & Associates Consulting
East Chicago Democratic Primary Mayoral Election
Call Sheet

District _____ Precinct _____ Logger's Initials: _____

Voters Name: _____ Phone Number: _____

	DATE	TIME	DISPOSITION	INTERVIEWER NAME
1	__ __ / __ __	_____	_____	_____
2	__ __ / __ __	_____	_____	_____
3	__ __ / __ __	_____	_____	_____
4	__ __ / __ __	_____	_____	_____
5	__ __ / __ __	_____	_____	_____
6	__ __ / __ __	_____	_____	_____
7	__ __ / __ __	_____	_____	_____
8	__ __ / __ __	_____	_____	_____
9	__ __ / __ __	_____	_____	_____

DISPOSITION CODES

Non-working or disconnected 0

Does not live in East Chicago (Terminate) 1

Not a likely voter (Terminate) 2
    (i.e., interview ceased after Q1 or Q2)

Business (Ineligible) 3

No Answer machine or answering machine 4
    (CALL BACK AT A DIFFERENT TIME)

Someone answered but the respondent not home or available 5
    (WHEN IS A GOOD TIME TO CALL BACK?) _____

Busy Signal 6

Refusal (i.e., will not take the survey) 7

Complete interview 8

Partial Interview 9

Other (Please specify) 10
    (OTHER) _____

WILL COUNTY SURVEY 1996: FALLBACK STATEMENTS
Thomas Roach & Associates

PURPOSE OF THE SURVEY

This study is being conducted to gather information about individuals who are active in Will County politics. The answers you give will remain strictly confidential.

CONFIDENTIALITY

Your responses to the questions in this survey will be kept strictly confidential. All results will be analyzed in the aggregate. When we look at the results of the study we will never identify your responses or those of any other person. Your cooperation is voluntary, but we would greatly appreciate your help.

HOW DID YOU GET MY PHONE NUMBER?

Your phone number was randomly selected from all phone numbers in Will County. By doing this we are able to give all people an equal opportunity of being selected for this study. I do not know your name or address, I simply have a Will County phone number. Your number will never be associated with your responses on this survey.

FOR WHOM IS THE SURVEY BEING CONDUCTED?

I'd be glad to tell you the names of the people who are sponsoring this survey when we complete the interview. The reason I am instructed to do this is that knowing who the sponsors of the survey are before conducting the interview may influence the way you answer the interview questions. However, please be assured that this interview is completely confidential and that your responses or any one else's, will never be made known to the sponsors of this survey. The sponsors will simply receive responses to the survey reported in the aggregate, that is, no individual's answers will be associated with their telephone number.

SURVEY SPONSORS

[DO NOT READ UNTIL THE INTERVIEW HAS BEEN COMPLETED]

This survey is being conducted for Jeffrey Allen, Daniel Kennedy, and Robert Lorz, all candidates for Will County Circuit Court Judge.

WILL COUNTY GENERAL ELECTION SURVEY – 1996

My name is _____, and I'm calling from Thomas Roach and Associates Research. We're conducting a short survey of Will County residents about national and local politics. The survey will take less than five minutes, and I would really appreciate your help.

May I please speak with someone in your household who is registered to vote?
{REPEAT INTRO IF ANOTHER PERSON COMES TO PHONE}

1. First, I need to confirm that you are currently registered to vote in Will County.

   YES 1
   NO 2   {POLITELY TERMINATE}
   DON'T KNOW 9   {POLITELY TERMINATE}

2. How likely is it that you will vote in the upcoming November 1996 general election? Is it . . .

   very likely, ... 4
   somewhat likely, ... 3
   somewhat unlikely, or 2   {POLITELY TERMINATE}
   very unlikely? 1   {POLITELY TERMINATE}
   UNCERTAIN. 9   {POLITELY TERMINATE}

3. I am going to ask you about some of the people who are involved in Will County politics. For each of the following people, please tell me whether you recognize their name or not. Please don't guess; instead, just feel free to tell me if you don't recognize them.

	YES	NO	DON'T KNOW
A. Stephen D. White	1	2	9
B. J. Jeffrey Allen	1	2	9
C. Gerald R. "Jerry" Kinney	1	2	9
D. Daniel L. Kennedy	1	2	9
E. Amy M. Bertani	1	2	9
F. Robert C. Lorz	1	2	9

4. In the upcoming general elections in November will you vote a straight Democratic ticket, a straight Republican ticket or will you vote for a mixture of Democrats and Republicans?

   DEMOCRATIC. 1
   REPUBLICAN 2
   MIXTURE. 3
   UNCERTAIN. 9

5. Now I have some questions about the upcoming Will Co. judicial elections. If the election for Judge of the Circuit Court: Twelfth Judicial Circuit, to fill the vacancy of the Hon. Edward F. Masters, were being held today, would you vote for Gerald R. "Jerry" Kinney, the Republican , or Daniel L. Kennedy the Democrat?

   GERALD R. "JERRY" KINNEY 1
   DANIEL L. KENNEDY 2
   UNCERTAIN 9

(continued)

6. If the election for Judge of the Circuit Court: Twelfth Judicial Circuit, to fill the vacancy of the Hon. Angelo F. Pistilli were being held today would you vote for Amy M. Bertani, the Republican or Robert C. Lorz, the Democrat?

    AMY M. BERTANI 1
    ROBERT C. LORZ 2
    UNCERTAIN. 9

7. If the election for Judge of the Circuit Court: Twelfth Judicial Circuit, to fill the vacancy of the Hon. Patricia A. Schneider were being held today would you vote for Stephen D. White, the Republican or J. Jeffrey Allen, the Democrat?

    STEPHEN D. WHITE. 1
    J. JEFFREY ALLEN 2
    UNCERTAIN. 9

8. Now I'd like to finish by asking you a few background questions to help us analyze the data. Generally speaking, do you think of yourself as a Democrat, Republican, Independent or something else?

    DEMOCRAT. 1
    REPUBLICAN 2
    INDEPENDENT 3
    SOMETHING ELSE. 4
    REFUSED/UNCERTAIN 9

9. What city do you live in, or are you closest to, in Will County? {CIRCLE ONLY ONE}

BEECHER. 1		MONEE. 12
BOLINGBROOK 2		NAPERVILLE. 13
BRAIDWOOD AREA. 3		NEW LENOX 14
CHANNAHON 4		PEOTONE. 15
CRETE 5		PLAINFIELD 16
ELWOOD 6		ROMEOVILLE 17
FRANKFORT AREA 7		SHOREWOOD 18
JOLIET 8		UNIVERSITY PARK 19
LOCKPORT 9		WILMINGTON AREA. 20
MANHATTAN. 10		OTHER _____ 21
MOKENA 11		REFUSED/DON'T KNOW 22

10. How many years have you lived in Will County? _____ YEARS

11. In what year were you born? _____ YEAR OF BIRTH

Thank you very much for your time, that completes the survey.

12. GENDER MALE 1   FEMALE 2

11TH CONGRESSIONAL DISTRICT PRIMARY SURVEY – 1994

My name is _____, and I'm calling from Thomas Roach and Associates Research. We're conducting a short survey of 11th district residents concerning local issues. The survey will only take about five minutes and I would really appreciate your help.

May I please speak with someone in your household who is registered to vote?
{REPEAT INTRO IF ANOTHER PERSON COMES TO PHONE}

1. First, I need to confirm that you are currently registered to vote.

    YES 1
    NO 2   {POLITELY TERMINATE}
    DON'T KNOW 9   {POLITELY TERMINATE}

2. How likely is it that you will vote in the March 15th *Democratic* primary election? Is it . . .

    very likely, ... 1
    somewhat likely, ... 2
    somewhat unlikely, or 3   {POLITELY TERMINATE}
    very unlikely? 4   {POLITELY TERMINATE}
    UNCERTAIN. 9   {POLITELY TERMINATE}

3 Now I'd like to ask you about some of the candidates who are running or have run for the U.S. House of Representatives in the 11th District. For each of the following people, please tell me whether you recognize their name or not. Please don't guess; instead feel free to tell me if you don't recognize them.

	YES	NO	DON'T KNOW
A. William "Bill" Barrett	1	2	9
B. John "Jack" Buchanan	1	2	9
C. Clem Balanoff	1	2	9
D. Frank Giglio	1	2	9
E. George Sangmeister	1	2	9
F. Daniel L. Kennedy Jr.	1	2	9
G. Dave Neal	1	2	9
H. Martin J. "Marty" Gleason	1	2	9

4 In the 11th District, seven candidates are running in the 1994 Democratic primary for the U.S. House of Representatives. If the Democratic primary election for the U.S. House of Representatives were being held today, would you vote for . . .
{REPEAT AS NEEDED}

    William "Bill" Barrett, ... 1
    John "Jack" Buchanan, ... 2
    Clem Balanoff, ... 3
    Frank Giglio, ... 4
    Daniel L. Kennedy Jr., ... 5
    Dave Neal, or 6
    Martin J "Marty" Gleason? 7
    UNCERTAIN. 9

(continued)

5. Now, I'd like you to rate your feelings toward each of the following people as either very favorable, somewhat favorable, somewhat unfavorable, or very unfavorable. If you are not certain, just tell me that. {PROMPT AS NEEDED}

	VERY FAVOR	SOMEWH FAVOR	SOMEWH UNFAVOR	VERY UNFAVOR	DON'T KNOW
A. William "Bill" Barrett	4	3	2	1	9
B. John "Jack" Buchanan	4	3	2	1	9
C. Clem Balanoff	4	3	2	1	9
D. Frank Giglio	4	3	2	1	9
E. George Sangmeister	4	3	2	1	9
F. Daniel L. Kennedy Jr.	4	3	2	1	9
G. Dave Neal	4	3	2	1	9
H. Martin J. "Marty" Gleason	4	3	2	1	9

6. There are many issues facing lawmakers in Washington today. In your own mind, which issues do you think are the most important for the U.S. Congress to deal with?

_____

_____

_____

      UNCERTAIN. 9

7. Here are some issues that people mentioned to us. For each one, please tell me whether you think it is *very important* for the U.S. Congress to deal with, *somewhat important*, or *not important*. If you don't have an opinion on any of the following issues, just tell me that. {REPEAT RESPONSE CATEGORIES AS NEEDED}

	VERY IMPORT.	SOMEWH IMPORT.	NOT IMPORT.	NO OPINION / DK
A. First, how about the federal budget deficit? Would you say this is *very* important for Congress to deal with, *somewhat* important, or *not* important?	1	2	3	9
B. And how about crime? (Would you say it is . . .)	1	2	3	9
C. Next, how about the economy?	1	2	3	9
D. What about reforming the welfare system?	1	2	3	9

(continued)

11TH CONGRESSIONAL DISTRICT PRIMARY SURVEY – 1994
(continued)

	VERY IMPORT.	SOMEWH IMPORT.	NOT IMPORT.	NO OPINION / DK
E. How about reducing illegal drug sales?	1	2	3	9
F. How about health care reform?	1	2	3	9
G. What about the quality of public education?	1	2	3	9

9. Do you think that the health care coverage provided to the American people should be nothing less than what Congress gets?

      YES 1
      NO 2
      DON'T KNOW 9   {SKIP TO QUESTION 11}

10. How strongly do you feel that way? Would you say . . .

      quite strongly, or 1
      not so strongly? 2
      UNCERTAIN. 9

Now I'd like to finish by asking you a few background questions to help us analyze the data.

11. Generally speaking, do you usually think of yourself as a Democrat, Republican, Independent or something else?

      DEMOCRAT 1
      REPUBLICAN 2
      INDEPENDENT 3
      SOMETHING ELSE 4
      REFUSED/UNCERTAIN 9

12. In which county do you live? {CIRCLE ONLY ONE}

      COOK 1   WILL 5
      GRUNDY 2   OTHER _____ 6
      LASALLE 3   REFUSED/DON'T KNOW 9
      KANKAKEE. 4

13. How many years have you lived in that county?

      _____ YEARS

14. In what year were you born?

      _____ YEAR OF BIRTH

(continued)

15. Finally, as part of our continuing research, we may want to call some people back and ask a few more questions. Would that be o.k.?

    YES 1

    {IF YES} Could I please have your first name, so if we call back we will know who to ask for? _____

    NO 2

Thank you very much for your time, that completes the survey.

16. GENDER MALE 1   FEMALE 2

352 Union Street, Joliet, Illinois 60433 (815) 723-1234

Spring 2001 Boater Survey Abstract

Summary: The majority of boaters chose the Hammond Marina because of proximity to home or work. Those who can compare their experience here to experiences at other marinas claim to be satisfied by an 8 to 2 margin. The areas of greatest concern are security, the handling of complaints, and seaweed control.

Significant Quantitative Findings:

Highest degree of customer satisfaction

- 81% satisfaction with office personnel
- 80% satisfaction compared to other marinas
- 80% satisfaction with customer service
- 77% satisfaction with harbor personnel
- (maintenance of ship store deli)

Lowest customer satisfaction

- 42% satisfaction that complaints were effectively resolved
- 51% satisfaction with security
- 54% satisfaction with hours of operation
- 56% satisfaction with portable pump-out service
- 59% satisfaction with fuel dock
- (maintenance of slip and beach areas)

Issues ranked from most to least important by boaters

- 88% stricter monitoring of main gate
- 86% additional evening security
- 86% additional security during events
- 84% frequency of dock walks
- 78% noise regulation
- 66% additional lighting
- 66% alcohol regulation

(continued)

Main reason for choosing Hammond Marina

- 77% proximity to home or work

Qualitative Data

- not a proportionate reflection of the quantitative findings
- seaweed emerged as a passionate concern
- other information elaborates on areas of lowest satisfaction represented in quantitative research

Recommendations for utilizing results of Spring 2001 boater survey:

1. Publish the results. This can be done by listing the survey questions and inserting the responses as percentages. This one or two page document can then be mailed to boaters or made available in a high traffic area at the marina facilities. It would also be useful to post or distribute the written responses. This lets respondents know that they have been heard.

2. Identify the complaints that can be quickly and easily addressed and act upon them. Document these changes and notify boaters that they have been addressed. Distribute or display this notice in the same manner used to distribute the survey results.

3. Stack rank other worthwhile issues that were raised by the survey and post them with a schedule indicating when they will be addressed. This process can be done with the assistance of a randomly selected committee of boaters. No reasonable person will expect the Marina to act on every request or complaint contained in the survey. Once boaters see that the results have been published and that many of their concerns have or will be addressed, they can be expected to be patient and cooperative.

4. Conduct focus group research to pinpoint concerns, and implement a second survey in approximately one year. The new survey should include many of the same questions to document changes in boater attitude. Some new questions can be added, but the repeat questions need to be identical to the way they were stated in the initial survey—this includes wording and punctuation. Changes to the original questions make comparisons problematic.

5. Organize teambuilding exercises for the marina staff. Comments in the returned surveys indicate that boaters perceive a disparity between those making management decisions and those who carry them out. This is probably the result of staff members expressing their own dissatisfaction or lack of identification with marina policy. Involving staff in the decision-making process is a good management practice, and it makes staff members more accountable for how they represent those decisions to customers.

Index